THE ESSENTIAL HAIKU

Crows Flying Through Snow
Yosa Buson; Private Collection, Japan

THE ESSENTIAL
HAIKU

VERSIONS OF BASHŌ, BUSON,
AND ISSA

*Edited and with
Verse Translations by*

Robert Hass

An Imprint of HarperCollins*Publishers*

HarperCollins books may be purchased for educational, business, or
sales promotional use. For information please write: Special Markets
Department, HarperCollins Publishers Inc., 10 East 53rd Street,
New York, NY 10022.

Designed by Debby Jay

Library of Congress Cataloging-in-Publication Data

The essential haiku : versions of Bashō, Buson, and Issa /
edited and with an introduction by Robert Hass.
p.   cm. — (Essential poets series : 20)
1. Haiku—Translations into English.   2. Japanese poetry—Edo
period, 1600–1868—Translations into English.   I. Hass, Robert.
II. Matsuo, Bashō, 1644–1694. Poems. English. Selections. 1994.
III. Yosa, Buson, 1716–1784. Poems. English. Selections.
1994. IV. Kobayashi, Issa, 1763–1827. Poems. English.
Selections. 1994
PL759.535.E88   1994
895.6'13208—dc20   93-40006
ISBN 0-88001-372-9

The text of this book is set in Stempel Garamond

Page 327 constitutes an extension of this page

06 07 RRD 10 9 8 7 6

For Leif and Margaret, Kristin and Cameron,
Luke, and Louisa

Contents

Introduction

THIS is a collection of versions of a hundred poems or so each by three masters in the haiku tradition, Matsuo Bashō, Yosa Buson, and Kobayashi Issa. It is a truism of Japanese literary criticism that the three men represent three types of the poet—Bashō the ascetic and seeker, Buson the artist, Issa the humanist—and their differences are clear at a glance when you read them. Here is a fall poem that has Bashō's poignant calm and spiritual restlessness:

> Deep autumn—
> my neighbor,
> how does he live, I wonder?

And this winter poem was Buson's painterly mix of precision and strangeness:

> Tethered horse;
> snow
> in both stirrups.

And here is a summer poem of Issa's, with its pathos and humor:

> Don't worry, spiders,
> I keep house
> casually.

Their careers span the great flowering of the haiku form. Bashō lived in the latter half of the seventeenth century, Buson in the middle of the eighteenth, Issa at the end of the eighteenth and the beginning of the nineteenth. Much of what has been done with this small form, they did.

All three of them were born in rural villages and made their way as young men to the capital, Edo as Tokyo was then called, to learn their art. Bashō came from a village in western Japan near Lake Biwa, Buson from a riverside village on the east coast near Osaka, and Issa from a mountain village in north central Japan. All three spent a number of years in travel, sleeping at monasteries and inns, participating in poetry reading and writing sessions in villages and towns, visiting famous historical and religious sites and natural wonders. Bashō did this in imitation of the monks and poet-wanderers of an older time, for whom travel and its difficulties were a form of freedom and a way of disciplining the mind. Buson and Issa took the same path, partly in imitation of Bashō. All three became professional teachers of poetry.

Their social worlds were different in many ways. Bashō is often referred to as a late medieval poet. He was born in the early years of the Tokugawa shogunate, which was a military dictatorship, a rule of generals that settled peace and imposed order on Japanese society and shifted the center of power from the old imperial capital of Kyoto to the Shogun's court in Edo. Bashō's father belonged to the landed gentry—the samurai class—and as a young man he had a gentleman's education that assumed knowledge of the Japanese and Chinese classics. He went into the service of the local lord as a retainer and from there to the city where he received the kind of patronage position in the bureaucracy that the gifted young of the middling well-born had been getting for centuries. He became, briefly, a clerk in the waterworks, a position at which he did not last long. In a short time, he became a popular teacher of linked verse, and then in his thirties he began his wanderings and wrote the poems and prose journals that contain his most original and subtle work.

By the mid-eighteenth century, some financial power had accumulated to the merchant class, the rice brokers of Osaka. Buson was a wealthy farmer's son, perhaps illegitimate. He had less social status than Bashō and a little more money—which he seems to have gone through. Finding his way to Edo as a young man, he studied acting, painting, and—to some extent in opposition to the intense nationalism of the government—the Chinese poetry and philosophy that had once been a part of serious education a generation earlier; though for Buson it involved a certain turning away from the commercial and chauvinistic spirit of his age. Buson also traveled, learning the painter's craft at which he earned his living. When he eventually settled down, he settled not in Edo but in the old, a bit out of the way, and still aristocratic precincts of Kyoto, where he became a well-known painter and, as an older man, a teacher of poetry.

Issa's milieu was more distinctly middle class. He was a farmer's son from a rural village in the mountains. He was raised in what amounted to a popular protestant Buddhist sect, the religion of lower middle-class farmers and shopkeepers, and he had his introduction to poetry from a village schoolmaster. As a boy of fourteen, he was packed off to Edo to become an apprentice and there entered a school that claimed—as most schools did by that time—direct links to Bashō and that practiced a kind of humorous, rustic haiku that appealed to the nostalgia of its largely urban, middle class audience. He became a formal teacher at the school in his early twenties, and—Issa was always something of a rebel—was asked to leave within the year, and set out on his own travels.

A word now about the form they worked in. The *hokku*, as it was called in Bashō's time, emerged, almost accidentally, from the practice of linked verse. It was, from the beginning, very attentive to time and place. It tended to begin with a theme from classical poetry—the poetry of the Heian court—that was associated with a season of the year. It then added an image that seemed to penetrate to the essence of the classical theme. The spirit of haiku required that the language be kept plain. "The function of haikai," Bashō once said, "is to rectify common speech." It also demanded accurate and original images, drawn mostly from common life. "The old verse can be about willows," Bashō also said, "Haikai requires crows picking snails in a rice paddy." He insisted on poetry as a serious calling. One of the fascinations of his life is that it amounted to years of immensely subtle thinking about how to give resonance and depth to the image, which he worked out in practice in his own work and with his friends and students. "A poet," he said, "needs to discipline himself every day."

The insistence on time and place was crucial for writers of haiku. The seasonal reference was called a *kigo* and a haiku was thought to be incomplete without it. In Bashō's poem quoted above, for example, the phrase *aki fukaki*, "deep autumn" or "autumn deepens" is traditional and had accumulated resonances and associations from earlier poetry as well as from the Japanese way of thinking about time and change. So does the reference to snow—*yuki*, which can also mean "snowfall"—in Buson's poems. It is always connected to a sense of exposure to the elements, for which there is also a traditional phrase, *fuyuzare*, which means "winter bareness." The practice was sufficiently codified and there was even a rule that the seasonal reference should always appear either in the first or third unit of the three phrase poem. Buson's poem—it is typical of him—violates that rule and an attentive reader might be led to ask what the connection is between the unexpected snow in the second line and the tethered horse or the rather mysterious snow in both stirrups. In the same way, the spiders in Issa's poem were a traditional mid-summer theme.

These references were conventional and widely available. They were the first way readers of the poems had of locating themselves in the haiku. Its traditional themes— deep autumn, a sudden summer shower, the images of rice seedlings and plum blossoms, of spring and summer migrants like the mountain cuckoo and the bush warbler, of the cormorant-fishermen in summer, and the apprentices on holiday in the spring—gave a powerful sense of a human place in the ritual and cyclical movement of the world.

If the first level of a haiku is its location in nature, its second is almost always some implicit Buddhist reflection on nature. One of the striking differences between Christian and Buddhist thought is that in the Christian sense of things, nature is fallen, and in the Buddhist sense it isn't. Another is that, because there is no creator-being in Buddhist cosmology, there is no higher plane of meaning to which nature refers. At the core of Buddhist metaphysics are three ideas about natural things: that they are transient; that they are contingent; and that they suffer. Though the melancholy of autumn is as traditional an experience in European poetry as it is Japanese, it is not fundamentally assimilated into the European system of thought. English poets had a word for these feelings, they called them "moods." When Wordsworth or Keats writes about being "in pensive or in wayward mood," you know that they're doing one of the jobs of the artist, trying to assimilate psychological states for which the official culture didn't have a language. Bashō's Japan did. The old Japanese phrase that sums up the transience of things, "swirling petals, falling leaves," was a religious thought.

Bashō's "Deep autumn" is a poem about the transience of things, and Bashō has connected it to a particular expression of spiritual loneliness. Buson's "Tethered horse" would, for Japanese readers, connect it through the image of a snowstorm to our mortal bareness, and the horse's tether would lead a reader to think quite naturally that suffering is a condition of creatures. Issa's busy spiders make their webs in a world peculiarly contingent on the whims of housekeepers with their own notions of useful activity, and they happened to be spared by the moods of summer, which in turn make the argument for a kind of compassion. All three poems represent quite traditional Japanese ways of thinking about being.

But what has fascinated all readers about them is that they are also something more, or other, than that. They have a quality of actuality, of the moment seized on and rendered purely, and because of this they seem to elude being either traditional images of nature or ideas about it. The formal reason for this mysteriousness is that they don't usually generalize their images. When the *hokku* became detached from linked verse, it also cast off the room the *tanka* provided for drawing a moral (though not all *tanka* do moralize, of course) and what was left was the irreducible mysteriousness of the images themselves. The French writer Roland Barthes speaks of this in *The Empire of Signs* as the haiku's "breach of meaning" and is able to make a post-modern case for them as deconstructions and subverters of cultural certainties. This case can be made, but the silence of haiku, its wordlessness, also has its roots in Buddhist culture, especially in Zen.

So much has been written by western commentators about the connection between haiku and Zen that I'm not inclined to say much about it here. A short version would be to say that Zen provided people training in how to stand aside and leave the meaning-making activity of the ego to its own devices. Not resisting it, but seeing it as another phenomenal thing, like bush warblers and snow fall, though more intimate to us. Trying to find this quality in every haiku, however, romanticizes them and the culture they came from. It tends to make one rush to their final mysteriousness and silence. I know that for years I didn't see how deeply personal these poems were or, to say it another way, how much they have the flavor—Bashō might have said "the scent"—of a particular human life, because I had been told and wanted to believe that haiku were never subjective. I think it was D. H. Lawrence who said that the soul can get to heaven in one leap but that, if it does, it leaves a demon in its place. Better to sink down through the levels of these poems—their attention to the year, their ideas about it, the particular human consciousness the poems reflect, Bashō's profound loneliness and sense of suffering, Buson's evenness of temper, his love for the materials of art and for the color and shape of things, Issa's pathos and comedy and anger. One returns to their mysteriousness anyway.

I thought that a book like this, that gathers together the work of these three poets, together with some of their prose and notes on the poems, would give a fuller sense of them to readers in English than has yet been available, and would also give some sense of the variety and intensity of experience this small form can sustain. What is in these poems can't be had elsewhere. About the things of the world, and the mind looking at the things of the world, and the moments and the language in which we try to express them, they have unusual wakefulness and clarity. Perhaps the best way to get to it, after one has familiarized oneself with the symbolism of the seasons and the Japanese habit of mind, is to read them as plainly and literally as possible. In the end, the best advice to readers of the poems may be the advice Bashō gave its writers: "Prefer vegetable broth to duck soup."

ROBERT HASS

THE ESSENTIAL HAIKU

I

BASHŌ

Portrait of Bashō
Hokusai

MATSUO BASHŌ

(1644-1694)

Bashō during his forty-nine years, reinvented the forms
of both the haiku and linked verse as they were practiced in
his youth and gave them a power and seriousness they had
rarely had before. The usual view of his career is that as
a young man in his twenties he wrote competently—the
work seemed brilliant to his contemporaries—in the re-
ceived styles of his time. By his early thirties he was a *hai-
kai* master and a professional teacher of poetry. Through-
out his thirties he studied Chinese poetry and Taoism, and,
at least for a while, he studied Zen and practiced medita-
tion. The poetry of those years, derivative at first, took
from the Chinese models a plainness and depth very differ-
ent from the rather showy and playful poems in the Japan-
ese tradition. By his forties, sick of literary life and of his
own role as a professional poet, Bashō began to travel—
there was a tradition of pilgrimage in medieval Japan as
there was in medieval Europe—and wrote the travel jour-
nals, mixtures of verse and prose, that have become classics
of Japanese literature. It was in these last nine years of his
life that he remade the haiku form, transforming it into one

of the great lyric forms in human culture and himself into one of the world's great lyric poets.

He was born at Ueno in the province of Iga, thirty miles southwest of Kyoto, the former imperial capital and still the home of the imperial family. Real political power was concentrated at Edo, now Tokyo, under the Tokugawa shogunate, which ruled Japan until the end of the nineteenth century. The world he was born into was still feudal, which is why, though a contemporary of Isaac Newton and John Locke, he is often spoken of as a late medieval poet. His father was of the samurai class, or a landed farmer with some of the privileges of that class. Bashō was the third child in a family of six. When he was twelve, his father died and he entered the service of a relative of the local feudal lord, or *daimyo*. He joined the circle of his master's son, Yoshitada, who engaged in the aristocratic practice of composing *haikai*, or sequences of linked verse, as a pastime. The dominant school of writing at that time aimed at an elegant witty style, full of allusions to court literature.

In 1666, when Bashō was twenty-two years old, Yoshitada died suddenly, and Bashō left the family service. Virtually nothing is known of his whereabouts for the next five years, except that he took the pen name Sōbō—"Bashō" came later—and that his poems continued to appear in *haikai* anthologies. Scholars guess that he went to Kyoto to study poetry and Zen. Tradition has supplied him with mistresses, though there is no evidence for this, and he himself said that as a young man he "became fascinated with the ways of homosexual love." In 1672, aged twenty-eight, he published a book, *The Seashell Game*, which is the record of a haiku contest he supervised. The book includes his comments on the poems, and the prose is witty and urbane in tone. Bashō moved to Edo in the spring of that year, probably with the intention of becoming a *haikaishi*, a professional master who could take students and correct verses for a fee.

By 1675, very much in the middle of the literary life of the capital, he had met Soin, founder of the Danrin school, which favored plainer language, mundane subjects, and humor. He also met important literary patrons and began to take students. In 1676, aged thirty-two, he collaborated with another poet on a haiku sequence, *Two Poets of Edo*, in the Danrin manner. He also visited his home and returned with a nephew, Tōin, aged sixteen, for whose care he assumed responsibility. In Edo, Bashō began work, which lasted four years, as a minor official in the waterworks. In the next year he and Sodo teamed up with a third poet to produce *Three Poets in Edo*, and he also did extremely well in a haiku contest. At the age of thirty-four, in 1678, Bashō was a recognized master, and a group of young men began to study with him and to form the circle with which he has been associated ever since.

Around this time, Bashō's studies in Chinese poetry began to deepen. Also around this time he shaved his head and became a lay monk. Two anthologies of his work and that of his students, including the well-known poets Kikaku and Ransetsu, were published in 1680; these had a distinctly Chinese flavor. And Bashō's withdrawal from the literary world of Edo began. Citing the Tang poet Po Chü-i on the virtues of retirement, he moved to a modest house—a gamekeeper's hut—in a more quiet and rustic part of the city. It was there that one of his students brought the gift of a banana tree *(bashō)*, which he planted in his yard. It is a rather luxuriant broad-leaved plant, and an exotic. It seems to have dwarfed the other plants in his small garden, and Bashō's poems suggest that he was very pleased with it. He took a new pen name from the tree and began to study meditation with a Zen monk named Butcho, who lived in the neighborhood.

In 1683, in a fire that destroyed much of Edo, Bashō's house burned down. From this vantage point, it would appear that the world contrived to serve him with a lesson in nonattachment every decade or so. His father died when he was twelve, his young friend and master when he was twenty-two. After the fire Bashō went to stay with friends in the country, then returned to Edo to supervise the publication of another anthology of the work of his circle, *Shriveled Chestnuts*, the afterword of which cites five masters: The Tang poets Tu Fu, Li Po, Han Shan, and Po Chü-i, and the medieval Japanese poet-monk Saigyō. While in Edo, Bashō had news of the death of his mother. His students took up a collection and built a new house for him, but in 1684 he began the travels—half homeless pilgrim, half literary celebrity—that occupied the rest of his life. And it was at this time, scholars say, that the overt Chinese influence began to fall away from his verse as his mature style emerged. The journey described in *Journal of Weather-beaten Skeleton* dates from this year. Bashō was back in Edo in 1686, and in late 1687 he set out on another trip, the one described in *Notes in My Knapsack*. In 1689, aged forty-five, he sold his house and began the journey that issued in his masterpiece *Narrow Road to the Far North*. During this long trip, or series of trips, his thinking about poetry centered on a sense of *sabi*, about which Professor Ueda has written so well in his study of Bashō; *sabi* signified loneliness, or aloneness, or the solitariness akin to no-mind, which gives intense concentration, and curious lightness, and a tragic sense to the work of this period.

At the end of that journey, in December 1691, Bashō returned to Edo. He was almost forty-seven years old and would live three more years. He thought about giving up poetry, but confessed that he couldn't do it. Though Edo literary life disgusted and seems to have exhausted him, Bashō was a beloved teacher and was gradually drawn back into that life. He moved into another, his third, Bashō Hut, where his students and friends transplanted the banana tree. In 1693 his nephew Tōin died of tuberculosis and Bashō undertook the care of Tōin's wife, Jutei, a Buddhist nun, and their three children.

After Tōin's death, in mid-August 1693, Bashō closed his door to visitors for two months. He emerged again in October and resumed his literary and social life. His health was failing, but he had a new poetic ideal, *karumi,* or lightness—"like looking at a shallow river with a sandy bed"—and was discouraged when his students didn't seem to pick it up. He left Edo on June 3, 1694, and traveled by litter to Ueno, then to Kyoto, taking Tōin's young son with him. There Bashō received news that Jutei, who was tending his house, had died. He attended a memorial service and composed a verse to her: "An autumn night— / don't think your life / didn't matter." He returned to Ueno, where his students provided him with a house and gave him a welcoming party. In late October he traveled to Osaka and met with students and followers. He was taken ill there in early November and died at the end of the month.

POEMS

Even in Kyoto—
hearing the cuckoo's cry—
    I long for Kyoto.

This road—
no one goes down it,
    autumn evening.

The whitebait
opens its black eye
    in the net of the law.

Felling a tree
and seeing the cut end—
     tonight's moon.

Autumn moonlight—
   a worm digs silently
      into the chestnut.

A snowy morning—
by myself,
      chewing on dried salmon.

A crow
has settled on a bare branch—
    autumn evening.

    On the way to the outhouse—
the white of the moonflower
    by torchlight.

The crane's legs
have gotten shorter
    in the spring rain.

First day of spring—
I keep thinking about
 the end of autumn.

Weathered bones
on my mind,
 a wind-pierced body.

Misty rain,
can't see Fuji
 —interesting!

As we walked along the Fuji River, we came upon an abandoned child, about two years of age and crying pathetically. I wondered if its parents, finding the waves of this floating world as uncontrollable as the river, had abandoned him here, thinking his life would last only as long as the dew. The child looked as fragile as bush clover petals that would scatter, today or tomorrow, in the first autumn wind. I took some food from my sleeve and threw it to the child as we passed.

You've heard monkeys crying—
listen to this child
abandoned in the autumn wind.

As for the hibiscus
on the roadside—
my horse ate it.

My brother opened a keepsake bag and said to me, "Pay your respects to mother's white hair. Now, your eyebrows look a little white, too."

It would melt
in my hand—
the autumn frost.

Many nights on the road
and not dead yet—
      the end of autumn.

The sea darkening—
the wild duck's call
      is faintly white.

Another year gone—
hat in my hand,
      sandals on my feet.

Spring!
a nameless hill
in the haze.

The oak tree:
not interested
in cherry blossoms.

At a shop for travelers:

A bucket of azaleas,
in its shadow
the woman tearing codfish.

A bee
staggers out
     of the peony.

When I looked under the hedge—
the little grass called shepherd's purse
     was flowering.

The old pond—
a frog jumps in,
     sound of water.

Harvest moon—
walking around the pond
all night long.

Awake at night—
the sound of the water jar
cracking in the cold.

Clouds of blossoms—
that temple bell, is it Ueno?
Asakusa?

Midfield,
attached to nothing,
    the skylark singing.

Clear water—
a tiny crab
    crawling up my leg.

Sickly,
but somehow the chrysanthemum
    is budding.

The winter sun—
on the horse's back
    my frozen shadow.

I don't know
which tree it comes from,
    that fragrance.

A petal shower
of mountain roses,
    and the sound of the rapids.

On the road:

> Tired,
> looking for a place to stay;
> hanging wisteria.

> The jars of octopus—
> brief dreams
> under the summer moon.

> Exciting at first,
> then sad,
> watching the cormorant-fishing.

Blowing stones
along the road on Mount Asama,
the autumn wind.

Seeing people off,
being seen off—
autumn in Kiso.

It's not like anything
they compare it to—
the summer moon.

A view of Narumi:

> Early fall—
> the sea and the rice fields
> all one green.

> As the sound fades,
> the scent of the flowers comes up—
> the evening bell.

> How admirable!
> to see lightning and not think
> life is fleeting.

A cold rain starting
and no hat—
    so?

The squid seller's call
mingles with the voice
    of the cuckoo.

By the old temple,
peach blossoms,
    a man hulling rice.

Spring rain
leaking through the roof,
    dripping from the wasps' nest.

Good house:
sparrows out back
    feasting in the millet.

Coolness of the melons
flecked with mud
    in the morning dew.

Moonlight slanting
through the bamboo grove;
    a cuckoo crying.

Singing, flying, singing,
the cuckoo
    keeps busy.

A cicada shell;
it sang itself
    utterly away.

The spring we don't see—
on the back of a hand mirror
a plum tree in flower.

Taking a nap,
feet planted
against a cool wall.

First winter rain—
even the monkey
seems to want a raincoat.

In the fish shop
the gums of the salt-bream
look cold.

Hailstones
glancing off the rocks
at Stony Pass.

Visiting the graves—
white-haired,
leaning on their canes.

Midnight frost—
I'd borrow
   the scarecrow's shirt.

Dusk
dims the hawk's eyes
   and the quail start chirping.

What voice,
what song, spider,
   in the autumn wind?

A calm moon—
walking home the gay boy
    frightened by the howling of foxes.

Not this human sadness,
cuckoo,
    but your solitary cry.

Sad beauty?
the morning glory—
    even when it's painted badly.

Having planted a banana tree,
I'm a little contemptuous
    of the bush clover.

Winter rain—
the field stubble
    has blackened.

First snow
falling
    on the half-finished bridge.

On the cow shed
a hard winter rain;
cock crowing.

The winter storm
hid in the bamboo grove
and quieted away.

Winter solitude—
in a world of one color
the sound of wind.

Awake at night,
the lamp low,
the oil freezing.

When the winter chrysanthemums go,
there's nothing to write about
but radishes.

The she cat—
grown thin
from love and barley.

Year after year
on the monkey's face
a monkey face.

A fishy smell—
perch guts
in the water weeds.

Wrapping the rice cakes,
with one hand
she fingers back her hair.

Su Tung-p'o, slanting his traveler's hat, would look up to-ward the cloudy sky, and Tu Fu, wearing a hat heavy with snow, would roam faraway places. Since I have plenty of time here at the grassy hut, I have made a rainproof hat with my own hands in imitation of the hat Saigyō wore in his solitary wanderings:

> Life in this world—
> a makeshift hut
> like Sōgi's.

> My summer robes—
> there are still some lice
> I haven't caught.

> The clouds
> are giving these moon-watchers
> a little break.

Mount Kazuraki:

> More than ever I want to see
> in these blossoms at dawn
> the god's face.

> The peasant's child,
> husking rice, stops
> and gazes at the moon.

> Heat waves shimmering
> one or two inches
> above the dead grass.

Spring going—
birds weeping, tears
    in the eyes of fish.

A village without bells—
how do they live?
    spring dusk.

The beginning of art—
a rice-planting song
    in the backcountry.

A HUGE CHESTNUT TREE on the outskirts of this post town and a priest living like a hermit in its shade. Perhaps like Saigyō, "deep in the mountains gathering chestnuts." or so I imagined and took a scrap of paper from my bag to write, "The Chinese written character for 'chestnut' comprises 'west' and 'tree' and is, therefore, linked up with Amida's Paradise in the West. This is why Gyōgi Bosatsu all his life used the wood of this tree for his walking stick and the pillars of his house."

> Chestnut by the eaves—
> not many people
> notice the blossoms.

> Summer grass—
> all that's left
> of warriors' dreams.

> Fleas, lice,
> a horse peeing
> near my pillow.

IN THE DEMESNE of Yamagata, the mountain temple called Ryushakuji. Founded by Jikaku Daishi, an unusually well-kept quiet place. "You must go and see it," people urged; from here, off back toward Obanazawa, about seven *li*. Sun not yet down. Reserved space at dormitory at bottom, then climbed to the temple on the ridge. This mountain one of rocky steeps, ancient pines and cypresses, old earth and stone and smooth moss, and on the rocks temple doors locked, no sound. Climbed along edges of and crept over boulders, worshiped at temples, penetrating scene, profound quietness, heart/mind open clear.

> Stillness—
> the cicada's cry
> drills into the rocks.

Wanting to sail down the Mogami River, waited for good weather at Oishida. Here the old seed of *haikai* had taken root. Still bearing flowers—it brought back past times, eased the heart, "the clear note of a reed pipe." But these country poets had gone astray trying to take both ways at once, new style and old style, no one to guide them. At their request, sat and composed with them, leaving a collection of no great merit. But further along than they were.

The river begins in the high mountains to the north, flows through Yamagata Province. Dangerous in spots, the Goten shoals and Hayabusa rapids. Descends north of Mount Itajiki and empties into the sea at Sakata. Came down fast, high mountains on either side, thick forest. The little boat called an *inabune* was used by farmers in the old times for transporting sheaths of rice. Saw the Shiaito falls plunge through thick green foliage, Sennindo Temple standing at the river's brink. The river swollen, so the boat ran risks.

> Gathering
> the fifth-month rains,
> the swift Mogami River.

A wild sea—
and flowing out toward Sado Island,
the Milky Way.

Staying at an inn
where prostitutes are also sleeping—
bush clover and the moon.

At a hermitage:

A cool fall night—
getting dinner, we peeled
eggplants, cucumbers.

Along the shore
mixed with small shells,
        petals of bush clover.

A caterpillar,
this deep in fall—
        still not a butterfly.

Fall going
and we part,
        clamshells on the beach.

Winter garden,
the moon thinned to a thread,
   insects singing.

From all these trees,
in the salads, the soup, everywhere,
   cherry blossoms fall.

The hollyhocks
lean toward the sun
   in the May rain.

They don't live long
but you'd never know it—
the cicada's cry.

The dragonfly
can't quite land
on that blade of grass.

Unchiku, a monk living in Kyoto, had painted what appeared to be a self-portrait. It was a picture of a monk with his face turned away. Unchiku showed me the portrait and asked me for a verse to go with it. Thereupon I wrote as follows—

You are over sixty and I am nearing fifty. We are both in a world of dreams, and this portrait depicts a man in a dream. Here I add the words of another such man talking in his sleep.

You could turn this way,
I'm also lonely
this autumn evening.

A group of them
gazing at the moon,
    not one face beautiful.

Cold night: the wild duck,
sick, falls from the sky
    and sleeps awhile.

At Shozui Temple:

A monk sips morning tea,
it's quiet,
    the chrysanthemum's flowering.

The Essential Haiku

To a prospective student:

> Don't imitate me;
> it's as boring
>   as the two halves of a melon.

> Wintry wind—
> passing a man
>   with a swollen face.

> Teeth sensitive to the sand
> in salad greens—
>   I'm getting old.

Very brief:
gleam of blossoms in the treetops
on a moonlit night.

Sad nodes—
we're all the bamboo's children
in the end.

Pine mushroom—
some kind of leaf
sticking to it.

The winter leeks
have been washed white—
how cold it is!

What fish feel,
birds feel, I don't know—
the year ending.

Bush warbler:
shits on the rice cakes
on the porch rail.

Cats making love—
when it's over, hazy moonlight
in the bedroom.

Harvest moon—
the tide rises
almost to my door.

All this foolishness
about moons and blossoms
pricked by the cold's needle.

The morning glory also
turns out
　　not to be my friend.

Still alive
and frozen in one lump—
　　the sea slugs.

The long rains—
silkworms sick
　　in the mulberry fields.

Coolness:
the clean lines
    of the wild pine.

Plates and bowls
dim in the twilight—
    the evening cool.

Lightning flash—
what I thought were faces
    are plumes of pampas grass.

Lightning—
and in the dark
the screech of a night heron.

This old village—
not a single house
without persimmon trees.

This autumn—
why am I growing old?
bird disappearing among clouds.

A field of cotton—
as if the moon
    had flowered.

Deep autumn—
my neighbor,
    how does he live, I wonder?

His death poem:

Sick on a journey,
my dreams wander
    the withered fields.

THE HUT OF THE PHANTOM DWELLING

(1690)

Translated by
BURTON WATSON

Beyond Ishiyama, with its back to Mount Iwama, is a hill called Kokubuyama—the name I think derives from a *kokubunji,* or government temple of long ago. If you cross the narrow stream that runs at the foot and climb the slope for three turnings of the road, some two hundred paces each, you come to a shrine of the god Hachiman. The object of worship is a statue of the Buddha Amida. This is the sort of thing that is greatly abhorred by the Yuiitsu school, though I regard it as admirable that, as the Ryōbu assert, the Buddhas should dim their light and mingle with the dust in order to benefit the world. Ordinarily, few worshipers visit the shrine and it's very solemn and still. Beside it is an abandoned hut with a rush door. Brambles and bamboo grass overgrow the eaves, the roof leaks, the plaster has fallen from the walls, and foxes and badgers make their den there. It is called the Genjūan, or "Hut of the Phantom Dwelling." The owner was a monk, an uncle of the warrior Suganuma Kyokusui. It has been eight years since he lived there—nothing remains of him now but his name, Elder of the Phantom Dwelling.

I, too, gave up city life some ten years ago, and now I'm approaching fifty. I'm like a bagworm that's lost its bag, a snail without its shell. I've tanned my face in the hot sun of Kisakata at Ōu, and bruised my heels on the rough beaches of the northern sea, where tall dunes make walking so hard. And now this year here I am drifting by the waves of Lake Biwa. The grebe attaches its floating nest to a single strand of reed to keep it from washing away in the current. With a similar thought, I mended the thatch on the eaves of the hut, patched up the gaps in the fence, and at the beginning of the fourth month, the first month of summer, moved in for what I thought would be no more than a brief stay. Now, though, I'm beginning to wonder if I'll ever want to leave.

Spring is over, but I can tell it hasn't gone for long. Azaleas continue to bloom, wild wisteria hangs from the pine trees, and a cuckoo now and then passes by. I even have greetings from the jays, and woodpeckers that peck at things, but I really don't mind—in fact, I rather enjoy them. I feel as though my spirit had raced off to China to view the scenery in Wu or Ch'u, as though I were standing beside the lovely Hsiao and Hsiang rivers or Lake Tung-t'ing. The mountain rises behind me to the southwest and the nearest houses are a good distance away. Fragrant southern breezes blow down from the mountaintops, and north winds, dampened by the lake, are cool. I have Mount Hie and the tall peak of Hira, and this side of them the pines of Karasaki veiled in mist, as well as a castle, a bridge, and boats fishing on the lake. I hear the voice of the woodsman making his way to Kasatori, and the songs of the seedling planters in the little rice paddies at the foot of the hill. Fireflies weave through the air in the dusk of evening, clapper rails tap out their notes—there's surely no lack of beautiful scenes. Among them is Mikamiyama, which is shaped rather like Mount Fuji and reminds me of my old house in Musashino, while Mount Tanakami sets me to counting all the poets of ancient times who are associated with it. Other mountains include Bamboo Grass Crest, Thousand Yard Summit, and Skirt Waist. There's Black Ford village, where the foliage is so dense and dark, and the men tend their fish weirs, looking exactly as they're described in the *Man'yōshū*. In order to get a better view all around, I've climbed up the height behind my hut, rigged a platform among the pines, and furnished it with a round straw mat. I call it Monkey's Perch. I'm not in a class with those Chinese eccentrics Hsü Ch'üan, who made himself a nest in a cherry-apple tree where he could do his drinking, or Old Man Wang, who built his retreat on Secretary Peak. I'm just a mountain dweller, sleepy by nature, who has returned his footsteps to the steep slopes and sits here in the empty hills catching lice and smashing them.

Sometimes, when I'm in an energetic mood, I draw clear water from the valley and cook myself a meal. I have only the drip, drip of the spring to relieve my loneliness, but with my one little stove, things are anything but cluttered. The man who lived here before was truly lofty in mind and did not bother with any elaborate construction. Besides the one room where the Buddha image is kept, there is only a little place designed to store bedding.

An eminent monk of Mount Kōra in Tsukushi, the son of a certain Kai of the Kamo Shrine, recently journeyed to Kyoto, and I got someone to ask him if he would write a plaque for me. He readily agreed, dipped his brush, and wrote the three characters Gen-jū-an. He sent me the plaque, and I keep it as a memorial of my grass hut. Mountain home, traveler's rest—call it what you will, it's hardly the kind of place where you need any great store of belongings. A cypress-bark hat from Kiso, a sedge rain cape from Koshi—that's all that hangs on the post above my pillow. In the daytime, I'm once in a while diverted by people who stop to visit. The old man who takes care of the shrine or the men from the village come and tell me about the wild boar who's been eating the rice plants, the rabbits that are getting at the bean patches, tales of farm matters that are all quite new to me. And when the sun has begun to sink behind the rim of the hills, I sit quietly in the evening waiting for the moon so I may have a shadow for company, or light a lamp and discuss right and wrong with my silhouette.

But when all has been said, I am not really the kind who is so completely enamored of solitude that he must hide every trace of himself away in the mountains and wilds. It's just that, troubled by frequent illness and weary with dealing with people, I've come to dislike society. Again and again I think of the mistakes I've made in my clumsiness over the course of the years. There was a time when I envied those who had government offices or impressive domains, and on another occasion I considered entering the precincts of the Buddha and the teaching room of the patriarchs. Instead, I've worn out my body in journeys that are as aimless as the winds and clouds and expended my feelings on flowers and birds. But somehow I've been able to make a living this way, and so in the end, unskilled and talentless as I am, I give myself wholly to this one concern, poetry. Po Chü-i worked so hard at it that he almost ruined his five vital organs, and Tu Fu grew lean and emaciated because of it. As far as intelligence or the quality of our writings go, I can never compare to such men. And yet we all in the end live, do we not, in a phantom dwelling? But enough of that—I'm off to bed.

THE SAGA DIARY

(1691)

Prose Translation by
ETSUKO TERASAKI

Eighteenth Day (Fourth Moon)

On the eighteenth day of the fourth moon in the fourth year of Genroku, we make an excursion to Saga and arrive at Kyorai's country house, Fallen Persimmons. Bonchō accompanies me. He stays until evening and then returns to Kyoto. I am to stay a little longer. The paper screen doors have been patched, weeds have been pulled, and a room in the corner of the house has been prepared as my bedroom. There is a desk, an inkstone, a writing case, and the following books: Po Chü-i's collected poems, *Chinese Poems by Japanese Poets: One by Each, Tales of Succession, The Tale of Genji, The Tosa Diary,* and *The Pine Needle Collection.* Along with these are various sweets arranged in a set of five gold-lacquered containers, stacked one on top of the other, with pictures painted in the Chinese style, and a bottle of vintage sake with wine cups. The bedding and relishes are brought over from Kyoto and are not lacking in any respect. I forget my previous abstemious existence and enjoy the luxury.

Nineteenth

About the middle of the hour of the horse, we visit Rinsen Temple. The Oi River flows in front of the temple, just to the right of Mount Arashi, and into the village of Matsu-no-o. The coming and going of worshipers to the Bodhissatva Koku is continuous. Amid the bamboo thickets of Matsu-no-o is one of the reputed sites of Lady Kogo's residence. There are three of these sites in the upper and lower Saga valley. I wonder which one is the real one. Since there is a bridge nearby called Horse-stopping Bridge, where Nakakuni of old is said to have paused with his horse, might it not have been this area? Lady Kogo's grave is in the bamboo thicket next to the small teahouse. A cherry tree has been planted as the grave marker. She, who spent her daily life in silk-embroidered garments and quilts, in the end turned into dust and compost among bamboo thickets. I am reminded of the willow of Chao-chun village, the flower of Wu-nu shrine of the old Chinese legends.

> Sad nodes—
> we're all the bamboo's children
> in the end.

> Arashi Mountain—
> the path of the wind
> through the bamboo grove.

We return to the house as the sun begins to sink. Bonchō comes from Kyoto. Kyorai returns to Kyoto. I retire early in the evening.

Twentieth

Nun Uko comes to see the festival of North Saga. Kyorai comes from Kyoto. Talks about the following poem, which he says he composed on the way here.

> Wrangling children—
> they're all the same height
> as the barley.

Fallen Persimmons House is unchanged from the way it was built by the previous owner, but here and there are some damage and decay. The present wretched condition is indeed more appealing to us than its previous polish and refinement. The sculptured beams and painted beams, too, are damaged by winds and soaked by rains; uniquely shaped rocks and pine trees are hidden under weeds. The blossoms of a single potted lime tree in front of the bamboo are fragrant, and they inspired these verses.

> Lime blossoms!
> let's talk about the old days
> making dinner in the kitchen.

> Cuckoo's cry—
> moonlight seeps
> through the thicket of bamboo.

> We'll come again,
> so ripen, strawberries
> of Saga Mountain!

The wife of Kyorai's older brother sends us some sweets and relishes. This evening Bonchō and Uko stay overnight. Since five of us sleep together under one mosquito net, it is difficult to fall asleep, and a little after midnight each of us gets up. Bringing out the sweets and sake cups of this afternoon, we talk until nearly dawn. Last summer when Bonchō slept at my house, people from four different provinces slept under a two-mat mosquito net. We all laugh when someone remembers that on that occasion someone said in passing, "Four minds, four dreams." As morning arrives, Uko and Bonchō return to Kyoto. Kyorai stays on.

Twenty-first

I feel somewhat poorly, from lack of sleep last night. The sky, unlike yesterday, is clouded since morning, and as the rain falls from time to time I sleep or laze around all day long. After sunset, Kyorai goes back to Kyoto. No one is around this evening. As I can't fall asleep, having slept during the day, I look for the scraps of paper on which I jotted down random thoughts at the Hut of the Phantom Dwelling and make clear copies.

Twenty-second

It rains during the morning. No visitors today. I feel lonely and amuse myself by writing at random. These are the words:

> Who mourns makes grief his master.
> Who drinks makes pleasure his master.

The fact that Saigyō composed the poem that begins, "I shall be unhappy without loneliness," shows that he made loneliness his master. He also wrote:

> In the mountain village
> who are you calling, yobuko-bird?
> I thought you lived alone.

There's nothing so intriguing as living alone. Chosho, the recluse, said:

> If one's guest enjoys a half-day's leisure,
> His host loses a half-day's leisure.

Sodo is always moved by these words. I, too, feel it.

> Not this melancholy,
> cuckoo,
> but your solitary song.

I composed this poem at a temple when I was all alone. In the evening Kyorai sends me some news. Otokuni is said to have returned from Edo with many letters from old friends and disciples. Among them Kyokusui's letter says that he visited the site of the Bashō Hut that I abandoned. He also has seen Soha there. Soha's poem:

> In the old days, who was it
> cleaned his pots here,
> violet blossoms?

He also writes: "Where you lived, there's nothing green except a single maple tree about two bows high."

> Young maple tree—
> your rich brown leaves,
> they last a season.

In Ransetsu's letter:

> Gathering bracken
> from among the shreds
> of ferns.

> The day for changing servants—
> to a child's heart
> a sad thing.

The other letters were full of touching thoughts, sentiments for which I feel a deep attachment.

Twenty-third

> Clapping my hands—
> with the echoes the summer moon
> begins to dawn.

> Bamboo shoots—
> they remind me of childhood,
> practicing brush painting.

> Ripening barley—
> does it get that color
> from the skylark's tears?

> Day by day
> the barley ripens,
> the skylarks sing.

> Having no talent,
> I just want to sleep,
> you noisy birds.

Bonchō gave this the title "Fallen Persimmons House":

> Tourists are also directed
> to the bean field
> and the firewood hut.

Toward evening Kyorai arrives from Kyoto. News from Zeze Shobo. Also from Shōhaku in Otsu. Bonchō comes. The abbot of Hompuku Temple in Katata visits us and stays overnight. Bonchō returns to Kyoto.

Twenty-fifth

Senna returns from Otsu. Fumikuni and Joso kindly visit.
Joso wrote *kanshi* in the Chinese style.

> Deep within Saga valley
> facing the mountain
> companion to birds and fish
> this sweet wilderness could be
> some old hermit's dwelling.
> No "red dragon's eggs"
> on the tips of the persimmon,
> but the leaves provide poetic themes
> and are conducive to learning.

And one called "Seeking Lady Kogo's Grave":

> She fled the imperial palace
> distressed by the strong reproaches
> heaped upon her.
> The autumn moon shines on her hut
> and the wind kicks up dust in the village.
> In a long-gone day the minister
> found where she was staying
> only by the sound of her lute.
> Where is her solitary grave now,
> among the trees and bamboo stalks?

Fumikuni:

> From sprouts
> they flourish into twin leaves—
> the persimmon seeds.

Joso, composed on the way:

> Is that a cuckoo?
> the nettles are as green
> as plums or cherries.

Made me think of a praiseworthy piece by Huang Ting-chien:

> Ch'en wu-chi, who sought to compose
> While closing his door to his friends
> And Ch'in Shao-yu, who exercised
> His brush in the presence of guests.

Otokuni comes and talks of Edo, also of a volume of *renga* called *Five-Bu Candlestick.* Among them:

> The lay priest's
> plaster bag
> in his bosom.

Kikaku:

> The mountain pass at Usui—
> wisest to use horses.
>
> Knapsack at my hip
> and a little mad in the moonlight.

Kikaku:

> Autumn storm—
> I handed over my cottage
> to the exiled man.
>
> Utsu mountain inn—
> borrowed a woman's nightgown
> and I slept.

Kikaku:

> Accused her of faithlessness
> and forgave her on Abstinence Day.

From around the hour of the monkey we have rain and snow and fierce thunder; it also hails. The size of the hailstones is about three *momme*. When the dragon passes in the sky, there is hail. The large hailstones resemble a Chinese peach, and the small ones are like Shiba chestnuts.

Twenty-sixth

Fumikuni:

> From sprouts
> they flourish into twin leaves—
> the persimmon seeds.

Bashō

> Rape blossoms
> scattering like dust
> across the fields.

Kyorai:

> A snail
> waving its horns
> uncertainly.

Joso:

> While someone else
> draws the well water,
> I wait for the bucket.

Otokuni:

> Morning moon—
> it must be the three-times-a-month
> mailman passing through.

Twenty-seventh

No visitors. All day I am at leisure.

Twenty-eighth

I start to say something about Tokoku in my dream and my profuse weeping wakes me.

When the spirit and gods intermingle, one dreams a dream. When the Ying-spirit dies out, one sees fire in his dream. If the Ying-spirit is weakened, one dreams of water. When a flying bird has hair in its beak, one dreams of flying, and when one sleeps on his sash, the dreams are of snakes. Dreams in Shui-chen chi, Huai-an kuo, Chuang Chou all have their logic and are not mysterious. My dreams are not the dreams of saints or princes. All day long I am filled with delusions and my attention wanders; at night my dreams are the same way. Dreaming about Tokoku is a so-called remembering dream. He was devoted to me and came all the way to my birthplace, Iga, showing his deep regard. We shared the same bed at night; we comforted each other after the fatigue of travel; he accompanied me on my journey like a faithful shadow for about a hundred days. Sometimes we shared our pleasure, sometimes our sorrows; feeling his sincerity permeating the depth of my heart, I have never for a moment forgotten him. Because of all this, I must have dreamed of him. After waking up, I weep again.

Twenty-ninth

I look at the poems on Takadachi of Oku Province in *One Poem Each*.

Thirtieth

"Takadachi soars into the sky resembling the star on a helmet—the Koromo River runs into the sea and the moon is a bow." The landscape described thus is rather different from mine. Unless one goes to the places, even the ancients could not make poems befitting them.

First Day (Fifth Moon)

Abbot Riyu of Meisho Temple in Hirata, Omi Province, visits me. Letters from Shōhaku and China also arrive.
Riyu:

> Unused bamboo shoots—
> on them
> some dew remains.

Shōhaku:

> These days
> summer underwear brings comfort—
> the fourth moon.

Shōhaku:

> Long awaited,
> the fifth moon nears—
> bridegroom's cake.

Second

Sora comes and says that he went to see the flowers at Yoshino and made a pilgrimage to the Kumano shrines. He also tells me this and that about my old friends and disciples in Edo.
Sora:

The road to Kumano—
as we go far upon it,
    suddenly the summer sea.

Sora:

Ōmine Mountain—
deep in Yoshino
    the last cherry blossoms.

Just about the time the sun begins to sink, we go boating on the river. We go up to Tonase along Mount Arashi. Begins to rain and we return home at dusk.

Third

The rain of last night continues unceasingly all day and all the next night. While we talked again of our friends, dawn arrived.

Fourth

Not sleeping last evening, I sleep all day, overcome with fatigue. The rain stops at noon.

Tomorrow it's my plan to leave Fallen Persimmons House, but feeling attachment for it, I take a good look at each room, in the front and in the back—all over.

Fifth-month rain—
poems pasted to the wall, peeled off,
    leave traces.

II

BUSON

Portrait of Buson
Matsumura Goshun; Private Collection, Japan

YOSA BUSON

(1716 – 1783)

Buson is that rare phenomenon, a great poet who was also a very distinguished painter. His poems are painterly in several senses. They are visually intense, many of them have a certain cool and powerful aesthetic detachment, and they are in love with color. There is a sense in them also of the world endlessly coming into being, as if it were brush strokes on white paper. In this his poems are something like the early poems of Wallace Stevens, and it is the Stevens of "The Snowman" and "Thirteen Ways of Looking at a Blackbird" who most resembles him among English language poets.

> Among twenty snowy mountains
> The only moving thing
> Was the eye of the blackbird.

Japanese scholars are fond of contrasting Bashō and Buson: Bashō the seeker, Buson the artist; Bashō the subjective poet, Buson the objective poet; Bashō the ascetic writer, Buson the worldly painter. These comparisons are relatively recent. After his death, Buson was known primarily as a painter. At the end of the nineteenth century the best of the modern haiku poets, Shiki, attempted to modernize haiku and wrote a series of essays on Buson, using him as a cudgel against what had become an indiscriminate cult of Bashō worship. Since then, Buson has been regarded as one of the masters of the form.

He was born, twenty-two years after the death of Bashō, at Kema, a suburb of Osaka, some thirty miles from Kyoto. His family name was Taniguchi; he took the surname Yosa—after his mother's home village—later in life. Not much is known about his childhood. He may have been the son of a well-to-do farmer and a housemaid, and he seems to have lost both his parents when he was quite young. In a letter written when he was in his sixties, Buson gives us a brief picture of the place: "My home village is Kema. When I was a child, on lovely spring days, I always went to the riverbank with friends and played there. There were boats going up and down on the water. On the banks were people coming and going, among them country girls who worked as housemaids in Naniwa and imitated the fashionable styles of that city. Their hair was done in the style of *maiko,* and they loved romantic tales and gossip."

What we know of Buson directly begins when he left home at about the age of twenty to study painting and poetry in Edo. There is a story that in his early years in the capital he squandered an inheritance and trained as an actor. He began his literary studies under Hayano Hajin, who had been a student of Bashō's disciples Kikaku and Ransetsu, and for a time was Hajin's live-in secretary. "Hajin rescued me from my loneliness," he wrote later, "and for several years treated me with deep affection." He also practiced composition in Chinese verse and attended lectures by the poet-painter Hattori Nankaku on Tang poetry and the Confucian classics. Buson published thirty-six poems in anthologies during these years and seems to have made his way in Edo's literary and artistic circles. Hajin died in 1742, when Buson was twenty-six; Buson left Edo and spent the next ten years wandering in the northern provinces, training himself as a poet and a painter.

But the years in Edo were crucial for the formation of Buson's aesthetic. He found his way to the tradition of Bashō in *haikai,* and through Nankaku to a group of poets and painters who modeled themselves on the *Wenjen-hua,* or literati painters, of China. Painting had been a trade rather than an art in earlier Chinese culture; in the *wenjen* tradition painting and poetry were brought together through the prestige of the art of calligraphy. The *wenjen* painters, from the Tang dynasty onward, elevated painting to a fine art through this alliance, and in the eighteenth century some Japanese painters began to take them as a model. Tokugawa Japan had closed itself to the outside world and did not look kindly on foreign fashions, so there was an element of dissent in this interest in Chinese art. The Japanese painters—called *bunjin,* after *wenjen,* or sometimes the Nanga school, after the Southern school of Chinese painting—used the *wenjen* sensibility to declare their freedom from the market in painting. It amounted to an art-for-art's sake protest against the commercialization of art by painters who nevertheless intended to make a living from painting. This movement was to affect Buson's career in a couple of ways. He made his living as a painter to free himself from having to make it as a poet, and as both painter and poet he found his way to traditions that resisted the vulgarization of the marketplace. In later years, a student asked if there was a secret to *haikai.* Buson said, in one of his few aesthetic pronouncements, "Yes, use the commonplace to escape the commonplace." The student then asked if there was any shortcut to learning how to do this. Buson said, "Read Chinese poetry."

During the ten years of his wandering in the north country, Buson maintained his artistic contacts in Edo and seems mainly to have worked at painting. Not much of the work from this period, either in poetry or painting, survives. He retraced Bashō's journeys, and later on made illustrated versions of *Narrow Road to the Far North* in the *haiga* style—quick, spontaneous drawings that have some resemblance to Chinese Zen painting. During this time, he stayed in a number of monasteries of the Jōdo, or Pure Land, sect, and, like Bashō, shaved his head and dressed as a lay monk. Jōdo Buddhism centered on the veneration of Amida, through whom, it was believed, one could be reborn in the Western Paradise. It was not monastic. Sometimes called The Easy Gate, it was perhaps the most conventional form of Buddhism in Buson's time. At least one scholar has argued that Buson thought about becoming a priest, but his interest in Jōdo waned in the 1750s. The religious sense in Buson's art, if that is what it is, comes from his love of Bashō's poetry and of the Ch'an Buddhist poets and painters whom he studied and admired; it's in his clear-mindedness and in his sense of the aliveness of things and of their presence.

In 1751, at the age of thirty-six, Buson traveled to Kyoto and stayed there, except for three years spent at Miyazu, a seacoast town north of the city, for the rest of his life. All the evidence is that he liked the life of Kyoto. He liked the theater—he even acted on occasion, he liked drinking with his friends, and he enjoyed the company of *maiko* girls. In 1760, at forty-five years of age and apparently sufficiently established as a painter to manage it, Buson married a woman named Tomo, who was also a poet. His letters—he wrote a great many of them—suggest a settled life. The *haikai* school of his teacher from Edo, Hajin, was established in Kyoto, and when its leader died, the Kyoto poets gathered around Buson and asked him to take the official title of the school's master. He was reluctant to do it and was quite contemptuous of the role: "These days, those who dominate the *haikai* world peddle their different styles, ridicule and slander everyone else, and puff themselves up with the title of master. They flaunt their wealth, parade their ignorance, and promote themselves by arranging their students' innumerable wretched verses in anthologies. Those who know better cover their eyes in embarrassment and are ashamed of such behavior."

But Buson did eventually succeed to the title, and, by 1770 or so, when he was fifty-five, he was the acknowledged leader of the poets of Kyoto and seems to have been making a modestly comfortable living from his painting. In 1771 he produced his most important visual work, a series of ten screens with Ikeno Taiga, the greatest literati painter of his time. Books of Buson's poems appeared, *Light from the Snow* in 1772 and *Around Here* and *A Crow at Dawn* in 1773. During the last ten years of his life, Buson married his daughter to the son of the cook for an Osaka millionaire (then, as now, poets and chefs must have had about the same social position), announced in a letter to a friend that he was going to forswear romantic attachment to geishas for the sake of his dignity in old age, wrote his major prose work, published his experiments in the long poem, took a trip to paint the mountains at Yoshino, extricated his daughter from the marriage when it didn't work out (the groom's father, he said, was mercenary), received friends and students (though one of his recorded aphorisms is "On the whole, it is a bother to keep up relationships with people in this world"), and wrote an essay on mushroom gathering. In 1783 he suffered chest pains and died, at the age of fifty-nine.

Buson's young friend Kitō left an account of his last days. There was a moment when he turned to his night nurse and said, "Even being sick like this, my fondness for the way is beyond reason and I try to make haiku. The high stage of 'My dream hovers over withered fields' (Bashō's last poem) is impossible for me to reach. Therefore, the old poet Bashō's greatness is supremely moving to me now." Like Bashō, Buson died at the end of winter, but he called his last poem, dictated to a friend, "Early Spring." It describes the plum blossoms in his garden just beginning to whiten in the light before sunrise.

POEMS

Haiku (*Yomeiride* by Matsumura Goshun)
Yosa Buson; Itsuo Museum, Ikeda

I go,
you stay;
two autumns.

The two plum trees—
I love their blooming!
one early, one later.

Coolness—
the sound of the bell
as it leaves the bell.

White blossoms of the pear
and a woman in moonlight
    reading a letter.

    Green leaves,
white water,
    the barley yellowing.

    Tea flowers—
are they white?
    yellow?

Coming back—
so many pathways
    through the spring grass.

Tilling the field;
the man who asked the way
    has disappeared.

Fallen petals of red plum—
they seem to be burning
    on the clods of horse shit.

Plums in blossom
and the geishas who can't go out
are buying sashes.

The old cormorant keeper—
I haven't seen him
this year.

Apprentice's day off:
hops over a kite string,
keeps going.

Lighting one candle
with another candle—
    spring evening.

Listening to the lute one spring evening:

    Tears
for the wild geese of Shosho;
    a hazy moon.

    That snail—
one long horn, one short,
    what's on his mind?

Around the small house
struck by lightning,
        melon flowers.

The spring sea rising
and falling, rising
        and falling all day.

Ploughing the land—
not even a bird singing
        in the mountain's shadow.

How awkward it looks
swimming—
    the frog.

Early summer rain—
houses facing the river,
    two of them.

Sparrow singing—
its tiny mouth
    open.

Sick man passing
in a palanquin; summer
    is the autumn of barley.

The cherry blossoms fallen—
through the branches
    a temple.

At a place called Kaya:

Crossing
the summer river,
    sandals in my hand.

They end their flight
one by one—
    crows at dusk.

His Holiness the Abbot
is shitting
    in the withered fields.

Blow of an ax,
pine scent,
    the winter woods.

Sound of a saw;
poor people,
    winter midnight.

Going home,
the horse stumbles
    in the winter wind.

Straw sandal half sunk
in an old pond
    in the sleety snow.

A field of mustard,
no whale in sight,
    the sea darkening.

Blown from the west,
fallen leaves gather
    in the east.

Autumn evening—
there's joy also
    in loneliness.

Two Crows in Winter
Yosa Buson; Private Collection, Japan

Field of bright mustard,
the moon in the east,
    the sun in the west.

The mad girl
in the boat at midday;
    spring currents.

Washing the hoe—
ripples on the water;
    far off, wild ducks.

In the drained fields
how long and thin
    the legs of the scarecrow.

Green plum—
it draws her eyebrows
    together.

The sound of a bell
struck off center
    vanishes in haze.

Riding
a short-legged horse
in the hazy spring.

Night deepens,
sleep in the villages,
the sound of falling water.

A urine-stained quilt
drying on the line—
Suma village.

The short night—
on the hairy caterpillar
    beads of dew.

The short night—
patrolmen
    washing in the river.

The short night—
bubbles of crab froth
    among the river reeds.

The short night—
a broom thrown away
on the beach.

The short night—
the Oi River
has sunk two feet.

The short night—
on the outskirts of the village
a small shop opening.

The short night—
broken, in the shallows,
   a crescent moon.

The short night—
the peony
   has opened.

The short night—
waves beating in,
   an abandoned fire.

The short night—
near the pillow
a screen turning silver.

The short night—
shallow footprints
on the beach at Yui.

Evening wind:
water laps
the heron's legs.

Dawn—
fish the cormorants haven't caught
swimming in the shallows.

Chrysanthemum growers—
you are the slaves
of chrysanthemums!

A heavy cart rumbles by
and the peonies
quiver.

They swallow clouds
and spit out blossoms—
　　the Yoshino Mountains.

Light of the moon
moves west, flowers' shadows
　　creep eastward.

He's on the porch,
to escape the wife and kids—
　　how hot it is!

Landscapes of the Four Seasons (detail)
Yosa Buson

A flying squirrel
chewing on a bird
in the withered fields.

A day slow in going
echoes
in the corners of Kyoto.

White dew—
one drop
on each thorn.

Not quite dark yet
and the stars shining
    above the withered fields.

Buying leeks
and walking home
    under the bare trees.

Cover my head
or my feet?
    the winter quilt.

A bat flits
in moonlight
above the plum blossoms.

Peonies scattering,
two or three petals
lie on one another.

A moored boat;
where
did the spring go?

Misty grasses,
quiet waters,
    it's evening.

Brushing flies
from the sick girl in the palanquin—
    how hot it is!

In the summer rain
the path
    has disappeared.

Leaves some trout,
knocks, goes on,
    the evening gate.

A dog barking
at a peddler:
    peach trees in bloom.

The owner of the field
goes to see how his scarecrow is
    and comes back.

Butterfly
sleeping
on the temple bell.

The lights are going out
in the doll shops—
spring rain.

Evening primrose—
there ought to be
a yellow kind.

No bridge
and the sun going down—
      spring currents.

Bats flitting here and there;
the woman across the street
      glances this way.

Wading through it
her feet muddied
      the spring current.

When old Unribo was staying in Edo, in Nakabushi, he bought a keg of rice wine and a year's supply of grain and kept himself in complete isolation. In the summers he composed haiku every day and kept them in a notebook.

Remembering how
he holed up to write all summer—
how fragrant my ink smells!

The willow leaves fallen,
the spring gone dry,
rocks here and there.

The petals fall
and the river takes them—
plum tree on the bank.

Listening to the plovers
while you, who loaned me this room,
are sleeping.

By moonlight
the blossoming plum
is a tree in winter.

Sleeping late—
stuck to the soles of his sandals,
cherry blossoms.

Lighting the lantern—
the yellow chrysanthemums
lose their color.

Having reddened the plum blossoms,
the sunset attacks
oaks and pines.

Makes the eye happy—
the whiteness
of the lover's fan.

Morning breeze
riffling
the caterpillar's hair.

May rains—
even a nameless stream
is a frightening thing.

Flowers offered to the Buddha
come floating
down the winter river.

A shortcut:
up to my knees
   in summer rain.

Old well,
a fish leaps—
   dark sound.

Sudden shower—
a flock of sparrows
   clinging to the grasses.

The mountain cuckoo—
born, I suppose,
    in the crotch of a tree.

The mountain cuckoo—
don't know what
    it lives on.

The behavior of the pigeon
is beyond reproach,
    but the mountain cuckoo?

Not a leaf stirring;
frightening,
the summer grove.

Escaped the nets,
escaped the ropes—
moon on the water.

The old man
cutting barley—
bent like a sickle.

Plum blossoms here and there—
it's good to go north,
       good to go south.

Calligraphy of geese
against the sky—
       the moon seals it.

It cried three times,
the deer,
       then silence.

A tub with no bottom
blowing around
    in the autumn wind.

The end of spring—
the poet is brooding
    about editors.

The camellia—
it fell into the darkness
    of the old well.

Harvest moon—
called at his house,
     he was digging potatoes.

Crossing the autumn moor—
I keep hearing
     someone behind me!

Gleaning the rice field—
they work toward
     the sunny places.

Three Crows on a Pine Bough
Yosa Buson; Shogoro Yabumoto, Hyogo

The mason's finger
bleeds
near azaleas.

Before the white chrysanthemum
the scissors hesitate
a moment.

My arm for a pillow,
I really like myself
under the hazy moon.

People visiting all day—
in between
        the quiet of the peony.

An iris
spattered with the droppings
        of a hawk.

The end of spring
lingers
        in the cherry blossoms.

My old man's ears—
summer rain
   gurgling down the drainpipe.

Village with a thousand eaves
and sounds of the market
   in the morning mist.

Listening to the moon,
gazing at the croaking of frogs
   in a field of ripe rice.

Cut the peony—
nothing left
     in the garden.

The old calendar
fills me with gratitude
     like a sutra.

A tethered horse,
snow
     in both stirrups.

A gust of wind
whitens
the water birds.

On his deathbed:

Winter warbler—
long ago in Wang Wei's
hedge also.

Early spring:

In the white plum blossoms
night to next day
just turning.

LONG POEMS

Mourning for Hokuju Rosen

You left in the morning. Tonight my heart is in a
        thousand pieces.
Why are you far away?

Thinking of you I go to the hillside and wander.
The hillside—why is it so saddening?

Yellow of dandelions, the shepherd's purse blooming
        white.
There's no one to look at them.

A pheasant calls and calls without stopping.
I had a friend. We lived with a river between us.

Smoke rises, the west wind blowing so hard
in the fields of bamboo grass and sedge
it doesn't linger.

I had a friend. We lived with a river between us.
Not even the birds call out *hororo*.

You left in the morning. Tonight my heart is in a
        thousand pieces.
Why are you far away?

By the image of Amida I light no candle
and offer no flowers. I sit here alone,
my heart heavy, filled with gratitude.

Buson

Song of the Yodo River

She speaks (in Chinese verse):

Plum blossoms float by on the spring water,
flowing south where the Uji meets the Yodo.
Don't cut the mooring rope.
Your boat will be lightning in the rapids.

Where the Uji joins the Yodo,
and they flow together as one body,
I want to lie down in the boat with you,
and when I grow old be with you in Naniwa.

*He speaks (in a Chinese quatrain composed
in Japanese):*

You are plum blossoms on the water.
petals floating by till they pass out of sight.
I am a willow growing by the stream.
My shadow is sunk in it, and I cannot follow.

Spring Wind on the Riverbank at Kema

One day I went to visit an old friend in my home country. I had crossed the Yodo River and was walking along the Kema riverbank when I happened to catch up with a young woman on her way home for a visit. We passed one another from time to time for some distance and began to talk a little. She was beautiful—elegant and charmingly sensuous. Afterward I made a song of eighteen parts, in which I tried to speak her thoughts and feelings.

1

New Year's holiday
I set out from Naniwa—
    the Nagara River!

2

Spring wind—
the river bank goes on and on
    and home is still far away.

3

Leaving the bank to the sweet grasses,
the thorny bushes block my way.
Why are you jealous, thorns,
tearing at the hem of my robe, scratching my legs?

4

Rocks are scattered in the stream.
I step on them, picking the fragrant cresses.
Thank you, rocks in the water,
For keeping my trailing robe quite dry.

5

A solitary teahouse—
the willow beside it
has grown old!

6

The old woman in the tea shop greets me profusely.
She is glad I am well, admires my spring robe.

7

Two men are sitting inside, speaking
the language of the southern riverside.
They leave three strings of coins behind,
and offer me their bench when they go.

8

Old farmhouses, two or three—
a cat calls for his mate,
but no mate comes.

9

Outside the fence a hen calls her fledglings.
The grass is quite green all around her.
The chicks rush to her call, fluttering.
But they keep falling back from the high fence.

10

Three paths through the high spring grass—
one is quicker and I take it.

11

Dandelions blooming—three and three, five and five.
Five and five—yellow. Three and three—white.
I remember that, another time, I took this road.

12

Endearing flower: I pick a dandelion,
White milk spilling from the short stem.

13

Long, long ago
my mother's tender care—
    I think of it eagerly.

    Held close to her breast—
That was another kind of springtime.

14

Springs passed, I grew up and went to Naniwa.
The plum blossoms were white by Naniwa bridge
        in my master's rich house.
And I grew used to the ways of Naniwa.

15

Three springs now since leaving my home
    neglecting my brother.

A grafted plum that forgot its roots,
    blossoming on a strange branch.

16

Here the springtime has deepened.
       I go on and on,
       go on and on.

The bank lined with willows dips slowly.

17

Raising my head I catch a first glimpse,
    my home and garden in the dusk.

Leaning against the door the one with white hair
    holding my brother and waiting for me,
       spring after spring.

18

Do you remember the haiku of Taiga?

> "New Year's holiday—
> she sleeps beside the mother
>   whom she left alone."

FROM *NEW FLOWER PICKING*

Translation by
YUKI SAWA AND
EDITH M. SHIFFERT

2

Once I stayed at a temple called Kenshoji, in Mayazu, Tango, for a little more than three years. One autumn, I suffered a fever for about fifty days. Inside the temple, at the back, was a large room with floor mattings. The doors were always locked tight; there wasn't even space for air to get in. I was in bed sick next to that room, and the sliding doors between it and mine were closed tightly.

One night, about two in the morning, my fever was down and I decided to go alone to the toilet. I got up onto unsteady feet. There was a long hallway that led past the shut room on the way to the toilet in the northwest corner of the building. With the lantern out, it was very dark. I opened the sliding door, and then, as I made a first step with my right foot, I stepped on something furry. I started, and tried to see what it was. There was no sound at all.

Though frightened, I tried to calm myself. I stepped out again, and this time kicked powerfully with my left foot at where I thought the thing was. There was nothing.

I was more mystified—shuddering, my hair standing on end. I went into the priest's room and woke him and his attendants from their sound sleep and told them what had happened. Everybody got up, and, with many lighted lamps, we went to the back room and looked. All the *fusuma* and shoji were closed, and there was nothing in the room.

Everybody said, "You have a fever. You say things that are crazy nonsense." They were annoyed and I went back to bed again, thinking I never should have said anything and feeling embarrassed.

When I was almost asleep, I felt a heaviness on my chest, as though a huge rock had been placed there, and I moaned and moaned. My cries woke the head priest, Reverend Chikukei, who came in saying, "Wake up! What's the matter?" He helped me to sit up and I told him what had disturbed me.

"I know what it is. It's that nasty badger." He opened a door and looked outside. Day was breaking, and we could see, plainly, from the hallway to the wooden veranda, a set of small footprints like scattered plum petals.

Then the rest of the people in the temple realized what had happened. They were very surprised, though they had ridiculed me for nonsense before.

When he had heard my moaning, the Reverent Chikukei had run to me with his sash untied and his kimono open in the front. Now his round testicles hung down like rice bags. White hairs grew over them profusely so that his important part was hidden. Since his youth he had had the itch there and was always pulling and scratching himself. He looked like that famous Shukaku priest did, dozing over the sutras.

I was embarrassed by my thoughts, but the Reverent

Chikukei laughed and recited the old haiku with its double entendre:

Autumn again—
Camphor wood of eight mat size,
   Golden Pavilion Temple!

(Hanging down—
   badger's balls,
   itchy balls!)

3

At Shimodate, in the province of Hitachi, there lived a man named Nakamura Hyozaemon. He was at the time a disciple of my late teacher Hayano Hajin. He took as his poet name Huko and was fond of *haikai*. He was the richest man in his neighborhood, and his luxurious house was two blocks square. For both front and back gardens he collected unusual-looking stones and trees; he had made a pond where he freed birds; his miniature mountain was regarded as a beauty of nature. Occasionally, the provincial governor paid visits there. Nakamura was a really rich man.

His wife, the daughter of a wealthy merchant named Fuji, was called Omitsu. She had had training in *waka* and stringed instruments, and had a gracious and tender nature.

Although they were rich, in time the family's influence declined and they were left to themselves. Few people came to visit. Around the time their fortunes began to slip, several strange incidents occurred. Among them was a fearful event that makes body hair stand upright. One year, in December, in preparation for the New Year, the family made more *omochi* rice cakes than usual and stored them in a number of large wooden tubs.

Each night some of the cakes disappeared, and there was much concern about who could have stolen them. They put a heavy wooden board like a door over each tub, and on top of each of these they put a large rock. The next morning they uncovered the tubs and half the cakes were gone, though the coverings were found in the same position in which they had been the night before. At the time, the husband was away on business in Edo. His wife, Omitsu, had been dutifully keeping house. She was a kind supervisor to the servants, and everyone felt sorry for her. There were tears of sympathy.

One night she was making the New Year's clothes out of beautiful silk. It was getting late, and she gave all the servants permission to go to bed. She went alone into one of the rooms, closed all the doors, and there, with a bright lamp, she sat sewing quietly. There was no sound but the dripping of the water clock.

At about two o'clock in the morning, five or six very old, withered foxes with dragging tails passed by in front of her knees. Of course every door and panel was tightly closed, not a chink anywhere. How could they have crept in? She watched them, startled. They moved as if they were crossing a field, passed in front of her, and disappeared, just faded away. Not feeling very frightened, Omitsu resumed her sewing.

The next morning someone called at her house and said solicitously, "How are you? With your husband away, you must be feeling uneasy."

Omitsu, looking even more beautiful than usual, told, calmly, the strange thing she had seen the night before.

"Even hearing about it," the visitor said, "gives me chills. How peculiar! Why didn't you wake the servants instead of enduring it all by yourself. Unlike a woman, you were very strong-minded."

"Not at all," she said. "I didn't feel the least bit frightened."

Usually rain at the shutter or a gust of wind in the shrubbery frightened her, and she pulled the bedclothes over her head. But on that night she had not felt frightened at all.

It was really a very strange thing.

4

There was an old poet, a disciple of Kaiga, named Hayami Shinga. One night when he stayed at the Nakamura house, he was placed in a front bedroom. It was the eighteenth night of the ninth month. The moon was clear and dewdrops were cool; crickets were singing in the front garden. The feeling of autumn was so moving that he kept the rain shutters open and went to bed with only the paper doors closed.

At about one o'clock he happened to lift his head from his pillow and look around. The moon was still so bright that it looked like midday, and on the veranda, in a row, were sitting a number of foxes waving their round, hairy tails. The moon threw their shadows, plainly, on the sliding doors.

He was utterly frightened, and, unable to endure it, he rushed out into the kitchen, knocked at the door of the room where he thought his host was sleeping, and called out, "Please! Get up!" as loudly as he could.

His shouting woke the servants, and they began to shout, "Thieves, it must be thieves!" Their noise calmed Shinga, and, looking with fully awakened eyes, he realized that he had been knocking on the toilet door, yelling, "Get up! Get up!"

Later he talked of that night, saying, "It was very embarrassing."

III

ISSA

Self-portrait
Issa

KOBAYASHI ISSA

(1763 – 1827)

Issa—his name means "a cup of tea" or "a single bubble in steeping tea"—is a much-loved poet. He has been described as a Whitman or Neruda in miniature, probably because his poems teem with creaturely life, especially the life of the smallest creatures. He wrote hundreds of poems about flies, fleas, crickets, bedbugs, lice. His main English translator, a Scot, compares him to Robert Burns, who was almost his exact contemporary. There is something very like Issa in the tone of Burns's poem to the field mouse he turned up plowing: "Wee, sleekit, cowerin, tim'rous beastie, / O, what a panic's in thy breastie." And in other ways Issa's sensibility resembles that of Charles Dickens—the humor and pathos, the sense of a childhood wound, the willingness to be silly and downright funny, and the fierceness about injustice. Issa wrote thousands of poems, many of them quite bad, flatly didactic and sentimental, but in his best work he is—for all the comparisons—quite unlike anyone else, the laughter cosmic, the sense of pain intense, as if the accuracy and openness of his observation left him with a thinness of the mind's skin, with no defenses against the suffering in the world. Though he was a pious

Buddhist and inclined to moralize in his prose, there is an interesting edge of rage in his poems, something very near cynicism. What is delightful about his insouciance casts a shadow.

Issa's milieu was middle class. He was born Yataro Kobayashi in 1763, in the small mountain village of Kashiwabara in the province of Shinano in central Japan, the first son of a farmer with literary tastes. His mother died when he was two years old, an event that was to mark his life, and he was raised mostly by his grandmother. He attended the village school, where he was taught by a schoolmaster who kept the staging inn, practiced calligraphy, and wrote haiku under the name of Shimpo. Issa's father married a woman named Satsu when Issa was eight years old. When Issa was nine, Satsu bore a son, Senroku, and a bitter struggle began between son and stepmother that was to last much of Issa's life. His grandmother died when he was fourteen, and the following year his father, perhaps to end the conflict in the family, hired him out as an apprentice and sent him to Edo. His father traveled with him on part of his journey from home, and, according to the Scots translator, gave him final words of advice at parting: "Eat nothing harmful, don't let people think ill of you, and let me soon see your bonny face again."

Not much is known of what happened to Issa in his first ten years in the capital. By the time he was twenty-five, however, he was studying haiku under a man named Chikua and was publishing poems in the anthologies of Chikua's group, which was known as the Katsushika school and claimed an attachment to the tradition of Bashō. Although he was aware of Buson's work and wrote some imitations of it, it was the Danrin-like style of the Chikua group that formed Issa's own style. One scholar described that style as a reaching back past Bashō to get to

Bashō. Later, Issa described what the group wrote as "countrified *haikai*." But several elements of their style, the address to animals, lots of onomatopoeia, and more vernacular language than was used by either Bashō or Buson, as well as local slang, became part of Issa's characteristic idiom.

Issa's gift must have been recognized, because three years after joining the group, when Chikua died, he became the master at Chikua's Edo house, Nirokuan. Issa's tenure lasted just a year—apparently there were complaints against him from the more orthodox group members—and at age twenty-nine he resigned his position, returned to Kashiwabara to visit his father, and then—on the model of Saigyō and Bashō—set out on travels that were to occupy him for the next ten years. At this time he took the name Issa and adopted the tonsure. Following a common practice among teachers, he wore priestly garb for the rest of his life. Like Buson, Issa was a Pure Land Buddhist, though the sect in which he was raised, now the most numerous in Japan, seems, in western terms, distinctly protestant, pious, attentive to worldly work, and centered, in an almost Calvinist way, on faith.

Apparently Issa had some financial support from his father for his travels, and he made his living as an itinerant *haikaishi*, composing *renga* with local groups and correcting verses. He went south first to Ise, Nara, Kyoto, where he made offerings at the Hogangji Temple at his father's request, Oska, the tomb of Bashō on the shore of Lake Biwa, and the island of Shikoku. In 1796 he traveled to the south again, then returned to Edo in 1798—the year of Wordsworth's *Lyrical Ballads*—and published his travel journals. In 1799 he made a third trip through the central mountains to the coast of the Sea of Japan.

In 1801 his father fell ill with typhus just after Issa had

returned to Kashiwabara to visit, and Issa nursed the old man in the month before his death. His father left a will, giving him the main part of his property on the condition that Issa settle there and marry. His stepmother and stepbrother refused to recognize the will, and the villagers, who had been their neighbors for years, supported them. Issa left a record of this time, *A Journal of My Father's Last Days*, which reads something like a chapter from a novel by Balzac.

The conflict initiated a new phase in Issa's life. From 1802 to 1813, he traveled back and forth from Edo to Kashiwabara while he engaged in litigation over the property. During this time he took students, and the stories about his Edo life, his casualness, his offhand way with the eminent, multiplied. Finally, the wrangling over his father's house was settled. Preposterously enough, Issa and his stepfamily decided to divide the house down the middle and live side by side. Issa is said to have composed a hundred haiku at his going-away party in Edo.

The last, catastrophic phase of his life began happily enough. He had returned to his home village and hired out his land to be worked. And he complied with his father's wishes by marrying a local farm girl named Kiku. He was fifty-one, and she was twenty-seven, and he seems to have been very fond of her. *Kiku* means "chrysanthemum," and Issa wrote a haiku about his young wife that can be translated as "Chrysanthemums / don't care / what they look like," or, "My Kiku— / she doesn't care / how she looks." A son was born in 1816 who survived a month, a second son was born and died the following year, a daughter, Sato, lived just over a year and died of smallpox. It was after this death that Issa wrote his major prose work, *A Year of My Life*. In 1819, Kiku was pregnant again, and after the delivery she fell ill and died. Her infant son did not live the year. Four years later, aged sixty-three, Issa married again, into a samurai family, but dissolved the marriage in less than a year. In 1825 he married a third time, a midwife named Yao. In 1827 the house that had caused so much contention and seen so much trouble burned down. That November, suddenly and without pain, Issa died, leaving behind his wife and an unborn daughter, Yata. Yata inherited the rebuilt house, and it was still in her family in the 1950s.

POEMS

New Year's Day—
everything is in blossom!
I feel about average.

The snow is melting
and the village is flooded
with children.

Don't worry, spiders,
I keep house
casually.

Bats flying
in a village without birds
    at evening mealtime.

Noon,
orioles singing,
    the river flows in silence.

Goes out,
comes back—
    the loves of a cat.

Climb Mount Fuji,
O snail,
        but slowly, slowly.

        Mosquito at my ear—
does it think
        I'm deaf?

        Children imitating cormorants
are even more wonderful
        than cormorants.

A quiet life:

       Under my house
an inchworm
       measuring the joists.

       What a strange thing!
to be alive
       beneath cherry blossoms.

       The man pulling radishes
pointed my way
       with a radish.

Deer licking
first frost
from each other's coats.

Moon, plum blossoms,
this, that,
and the day goes.

Asked how old he was,
the boy in the new kimono
stretched out all five fingers.

A dry riverbed
glimpsed
by lightning.

O flea! whatever you do,
don't jump;
that way is the river.

In this world
we walk on the roof of hell,
gazing at flowers.

Naked
on a naked horse
in pouring rain!

Don't kill that fly!
Look—it's wringing its hands,
wringing its feet.

My cat,
frisking in the scale,
records its weight.

I'm going out,
flies, so relax,
make love.

Even on the smallest islands,
they are tilling the fields,
skylarks singing.

Advice from a pigeon:

O owl!
make some other face.
This is spring rain.

Nursing her child
the mother
counts its fleabites.

Seen
through a telescope:
ten cents worth of fog.

Under the evening moon
the snail
is stripped to the waist.

Approaching my village:

> Don't know about the people,
> but all the scarecrows
>   are crooked.

> January—
> in other provinces,
>   plums blooming.

> For you fleas too
> the nights must be long,
>   they must be lonely.

This moth saw brightness
in a woman's chamber—
        burnt to a crisp.

Even with insects—
some can sing,
        some can't.

Blossoms at night,
and the faces of people
        moved by music.

If the times were good,
I'd ask one more of you to join me,
    flies.

The withered fields—
"Once upon a time, deep in the forest,
    lived an old witch..."

A huge frog and I,
staring at each other,
    neither of us moves.

All the time I pray to Buddha
I keep on
    killing mosquitoes.

Having slept, the cat gets up,
yawns, goes out
    to make love.

It once happened
that a child was spared punishment
    through earnest solicitation.

The moon and the flowers,
forty-nine years,
    walking around, wasting time.

The prostitute's shack
at the edge of town
    in the autumn wind.

Full moon;
my ramshackle hut
    is what it is.

Even a fleabite,
when she's young,
is beautiful.

One human being,
one fly,
in a large room.

Flopped on the fan,
the big cat
sleeping.

What good luck!
Bitten by
        this year's mosquitoes too.

        The toad! It looks like
it could belch
        a cloud.

        Red morning sky,
snail;
        are you glad of it?

The mountain cuckoo—
a fine voice,
and proud of it!

Evening moon—
they visit the graves
and cool off.

The bedbugs
scatter as I clean,
parents and children.

Napped half the day;
no one
    punished me!

She's put the child to sleep
and now she washes clothes
    under the summer moon.

Not yet become a Buddha,
this ancient pine tree,
    dreaming.

In spring rain
a pretty girl
    yawning.

    That gorgeous kite
rising
    from the beggar's shack.

    From the end of the nose
of the Buddha on the moor
    hang icicles.

That wren—
looking here, looking there.
You lose something?

Cricket
chirping
in a scarecrow's belly.

On my portrait:

Even considered
in the most favorable light,
he looks cold.

Washing the saucepans—
the moon glows on her hands
    in the shallow river.

Face of the spring moon—
about twelve years old,
    I'd say.

Not very anxious
to bloom,
    my plum tree.

A village named Little-Plum-Tree
and a bush warbler singing
on the shaft of a hoe.

Fleas in my hut,
it's my fault
you look so skinny.

The dragonfly,
dressed in red,
off to the festival.

Shinano—
as soon as the snow goes,
 the gnats arrive.

Zealous flea,
you're about to be a Buddha
 by my hand.

Ducks bobbing on the water—
are they also, tonight,
 hoping to get lucky?

The Six Ways:

Hell

> Bright autumn moon—
> pond snails crying
> in the saucepan.

The Hungry Ghosts

> Flowers scattering—
> the water we thirst for
> far off, in the mist.

Animals

> In the falling of petals
> they see no Buddha,
> no Law.

Malignant Spirits

> In the shadow of blossoms,
> voice against voice,
> the gamblers.

Men

> We humans—
> squirming around
> among the blossoming flowers.

The Heaven Dwellers

> A hazy day—
> even the gods
> must feel listless.

How *much*
are you enjoying yourself,
        tiger moth?

Hey, sparrow!
out of the way,
        Horse is coming.

No doubt about it,
the mountain cuckoo
        is a crybaby.

A good world—
the dewdrops fall
by ones, by twos.

Where
does cold come from,
O scarecrow?

Crescent moon—
bent to the shape
of the cold.

Napping at midday
I hear the song of rice planters
        and feel ashamed of myself.

They don't notice
the thief's gaze:
        the melons cooling.

That pretty girl—
munching and rustling
        the wrapped-up rice cake.

I'm going to roll over,
so please move,
cricket.

The old dog—
listening for the songs
of earthworms?

The crow
walks along there
as if it were tilling the field.

In the thicket's shade
a woman by herself
    singing the rice-planting song.

Plumes of pampas grass,
it's the helplessness
    of their trembling.

Visiting the graves,
the old dog
    leads the way.

In a dream
my daughter lifts a melon
to her soft cheek.

Spring rain:
a mouse is lapping
the Sumida River.

Autumn evening—
it's no light thing
being born a man.

No talent
and so no sin,
 a winter day.

A poor box;
four or five pennies,
 evening rain.

The cuckoo sings
to me, to the mountain,
 to me, to the mountain.

The holes in the wall
play the flute
        this autumn evening.

The fat priest—
edging out
        while he reads the last prayer.

This stupid world—
skinny mosquitoes, skinny fleas,
        skinny children.

Fiftieth birthday:

> From now on,
> it's all clear profit,
> every sky.

> Garden butterfly:
> baby crawls, it flies,
> she crawls, it flies.

> These sea slugs,
> they just don't seem
> *Japanese.*

Writing shit about new snow
for the rich
    is not art.

I envy
that child being scolded:
    end of the year.

Cuckoo singing:
I have nothing special to do,
    neither does the burweed.

The snail gets up
and goes to bed
    with very little fuss.

The flies in the temple
imitate the hands
    of the people with prayer beads.

Were it sweet,
it'd be my dew,
    his dew.

Mother I never knew,
every time I see the ocean,
every time—

Summer night—
even the stars
are whispering to each other.

Last time, I think,
I'll brush the flies
from my father's face.

With my father
I would watch dawn
    over green fields.

Not knowing
it's a tub they're in,
    the fish cooling at the gate.

New Year's morning:
the ducks on the pond
    quack and quack.

The world of dew
is the world of dew.
And yet, and yet—

The spring day
lingers
in the pools.

Under the image of Buddha
all these spring flowers
seem a little tiresome.

At my daughter's grave, thirty days after her death:

Windy fall—
these are the scarlet flowers
she liked to pick.

The woodpecker—
still drilling
as the sun goes down.

The evening clears—
on the pale sky
row on row of autumn mountains.

On the death of my son:

      Why did the wild pink break?
O why
    did it break?

      The pheasant cries
as if it just noticed
    the mountain.

    Its mother on guard,
the foal laps water
    from the pond.

Autumn moon—
a small boat
    drifting down the tide.

Here,
I'm here—
    the snow falling.

Pissing in the snow
outside my door—
    it makes a very straight hole.

The moon tonight—
I even miss
        her grumbling.

The new foal
sticks her nose up
        through the irises.

Her row veering off,
the peasant woman plants
        toward her crying child.

Insects on a bough
floating downriver,
    still singing.

His death poem:

A bath when you're born,
a bath when you die,
    how stupid.

FROM *JOURNAL OF MY FATHER'S LAST DAYS*

(1 8 0 1)

Translation by
ROBERT N. HUEY

Fourth Month, Twenty-third Day

A clear, calm, cloudless day, filled with the first songs of the mountain cuckoos.... As Father stood there, sprinkling water over the eggplant shoots, something came over him. He suddenly hunched down, turning his back to the early summer sun.

"Why are you crouching down in such a place," I asked as I helped him up.

Later I realized that this was a portent of the flower about to fade. It must have been an inauspicious day for my father; he had just said, "I'm feeling a little poorly," when he was suddenly struck by a high fever. His body was as if on fire, and although I offered him some cooked rice, he could not swallow a single grain. I was alarmed and wondered what could be the matter. I was at my wits' end, and for lack of anything else to do, I just massaged him.

Fourth Month, Twenty-fourth Day

Clear....I received some medicine from my friend Chikuyō. I urged Father to take it.

Fourth Month, Twenty-fifth Day

Cloudy, later clear....Father's illness has grown more serious day by day. This morning he couldn't even swallow rice gruel. About the only hopeful sign was that he kept down medicine administered a drop at a time. All day long he was writhing with pain and could only moan, "Oh, the pain! I can't stand it anymore."

How sad it was to watch by his bedside! It was more painful for me than if I had been afflicted myself.

Fourth Month, Twenty-sixth Day

Clear....I called the doctor, Jinseki, in from Nojiri to have a look at Father. His diagnosis was not promising. "His pulse is weak and irregular. Since he has typhus, the likelihood of recovery is only one in a thousand." I was quite out of my mind, as if I was sailing in a boat without a helmsman. Still, since I couldn't just stand there helpless, I forced myself to administer his medicine. My aunt from Nojiri stayed the night.

Fourth Month, Twenty-seventh Day

I was extremely depressed, and the rain that kept falling only deepened this feeling. I felt unable to go on living. Thereupon this came from my friend Chikuyō:

> Early summer rains—
> "Ah, yet more rain," I say,
> and gaze at the sky.

Fourth Month, Twenty-eighth Day

Clear. . . . As today was the anniversary of the death of the founder of our sect, Father was up early in the morning, and had begun to perform ablutions. I thought this would aggravate his fever, and tried to stop him, but he would not be dissuaded. Turning to the household statue of the Buddha, he began to read a sutra as was his usual custom. His voice was barely audible. I felt depressed as I gazed from behind at his ravaged form.

Fourth Month, Twenty-ninth Day

As my father's illness grew worse, he must have begun to worry about my future as an orphan, for he set to dividing his meager holdings in two between his offspring. With painful breaths, he gave his instructions. He said he would give the rice field at Nakajima and the one at Kawara to my younger brother, but Senroku did not seem to take kindly to this and grew hostile toward Father and his wishes. Father and Senroku quarreled all day. It all started because greed, perversity, and guile had blinded Senroku and had driven him out of his senses. How sad it was to see him turning his back on his father and revealing this world of men as it is in these evil days of the Five Polluted Ages.

This evening Father's pulse was exceptionally weak and I felt anxious about his being left alone. Although Senroku might not be a son who measured up to his father's expectations, I felt that, since he was blood-related, he would regret it if he were not at his father's deathbed. Concerned for my brother's feelings, I had him sleep next to Father. Turning toward Father's sleeping face in the lamplight, I lay there watching over his resting body. Throughout the night Father just gasped painful breaths, and it was hard to watch. I felt relieved when at last it became evident that the tide had turned and he seemed better.

Father had said that he wanted to try the bear gall medicine that the doctor at Nojiri was said to have at his place. Although it was barely two and a half miles down the road, I felt that were I to go and get the medicine, Father would not be properly taken care of in my absence since he and my stepmother had had a quarrel the day before. So, unknown to my father, I gave Senroku instructions and sent him off. The early summer rains had lifted overnight, but water was washing over the grass, making people worry about flooding in the rice paddies. And then Father asked where Senroku had gone. I could hardly hide the truth any longer, so I answered him truthfully. Father's rage was unsurpassed.

He fumed, "Why do you send him out to pick up the bear gall without consulting me? Even *you* slight me!"

From the bedroom, my stepmother seized the opportunity and, raising her voice, reviled me as though there was no one else around. She said things like, "It was that lazybones Issa who sent Senroku out without breakfast. Doesn't he care at all if his brother's stomach is empty?"

There was no way to remedy the situation so I suffered in silence. Pressing my head to the floor and wringing my hands, I repented tearfully of my error, promising, "I'll be more careful in the future." Father's rage abated somewhat.

Because Father's admonitions, whether given gently or in anger, were all for my own benefit, how could I resent them? But how pitiful was his weakened voice raised in anger. After I had spent the previous night brooding about our pending eternal separation, the joy of suffering Father's scolding this morning could hardly be surpassed even by the joy of a blind tortoise finding a piece of driftwood. Thus did the sun slowly rise higher in the sky, and Senroku came dragging his feet home.

Fifth Month, First Day

The sky stretched on, clear. Fresh ears of grain rustled restlessly; the lilies also suddenly came forth with their reds and whites. All around us people thronged to gather up the rice seedlings and plant the fields. Usually robust, Father was now unable even to get up, and looked very impatient about it. The day was so long, and from around midday he was grumbling, "Hasn't the sun gone down yet?" I could imagine how he felt. It was very moving.

Fifth Month, Second Day

Father took a turn for the worse. Although he was in great pain, my stepmother took no notice and was contentious as usual. Ever since the business of the distribution of the land, relations between my brother and Father had not been good. And although Senroku and I were of different mothers, I couldn't help but think that the real reason for his unpleasant hostility was that we had been enemies in some previous life.

Father felt bad about my not getting any sleep at night and kindly suggested, "Why don't you take a nap and catch up on some sleep, or go outside and clear your head a bit?"

Hearing this, my stepmother became as nasty as ever toward Father, criticizing his every fault and forgetting the Three Obligations. I realized with regret that my stepmother made even Father suffer like this because I, whom she despised, was in close attendance at his bedside. But where else could I go were I to get up and leave?

*   *   *

Fifth Month, Fourth Day

Father's condition took a definite turn for the better from yesterday and he looked quite good. My joy was boundless when he said he wanted something to eat. He seemed to have been revived by the medicine he had taken the night before, and when I fixed some *katakuri* gruel for him, he sipped up three or four bowls of it. Even Dōyō said that if this improvement continued, Father would soon recover; and keeping watch by the bedside I began to feel somewhat relieved. When Dōyō left, I saw him off as far as Furuma village. To the east and west the rain clouds were clearing and the sky was exceptionally lovely. The cuckoo proudly announced the season with its first song. Actually, the bird must have been singing earlier, but because my mind had been occupied day and night with administering to Father ever since he had fallen ill, today was the first day I really noticed its song.

> Cuckoo singing—
> for me too
> this day feels good.

> How refreshing!
> moon over this gate through which,
> at last, I'm free to pass.

*   *   *

Fifth Month, Sixth Day

Since the sky was clear and I thought that Father might be bored just lying around, I folded up his bedclothes and helped him to prop himself up on them. Then he began to talk about old times.

"Well now, you've been without your real mother from the time you were three years old. And ever since you began to grow up, you haven't been on good terms with your stepmother. Day after day there was fighting, night after night the fires of hatred burned. There wasn't a moment when my heart knew any peace. It struck me that as long as we were together in one place, it would always be like that. So I sent you to far-off Edo in the spring of your fourteenth year, thinking that once you were away from home, we might all be closer. Ah, if only I had been your father in different circumstances. I would have passed this house on to you after three or four years, making you settle down and leaving me free to enjoy my retirement. You must have thought me a cruel parent indeed to have hired you out as an apprentice while you were still just a young skinny-bones. I hope you'll accept all this as fate resulting from our previous lives. This year I had intended to make a pilgrimage to the sites of the Twenty-Four Disciples, and hoped that once in Edo I might meet up with you, so that even if I were to die from the rigors of the trip you would be there keeping vigil. But now, for you to have come all the way here and to have nursed me like this—surely the connections between us in our past lives could not have been weak ones. So even though I might die right now, what regrets should I have?"

Tears were streaming down my face. I just sat there, looking down and unable to say anything. Because of his kindness, my debt to Father is deeper than the matchless snows of Mount Fuji, unmelted by the summer sun, and deeper than a twice-dyed crimson. Yet I hadn't stayed at home and taken care of him. Instead, I had drifted around just like a floating cloud; before I could wonder whether I had gone east, off I was to the west. The days and nights rolled on like a wheel going downhill, and twenty-five years had passed. To have stayed away from my father's side till my hair was white as frost—I wondered whether even the Five Violations could be worse than this.

In my heart, I prostrated myself and thanked Father. But if I were to openly shed tears, it would surely make him feel even worse. So I wiped my eyes and said with a smile, "Now put things like that out of your mind. Just hurry up and get well." I gave him some medicine, and added, "If you get better soon, I'll become the perfect son of a farmer, the Yatarō you used to know. I'll cut hay, plow the land, and really set your mind at rest. Please forgive me for what I've been until now." When Father heard this, his joy was boundless.

*   *   *

Fifth Month, Eighth Day

Clear. . . . It was a day off from the fields, and a large number of people, relatives and others, having talked or heard about Father's illness, came to visit us. People came bringing buckwheat flour and sake, knowing that Father liked these things. He was overjoyed, and pressing his palms together he bowed formally. "Better one cup of sake when you are alive than gold piled high enough to hold up the Big Dipper when you are dead." Anyone, whether from China or Japan, can sympathize with this sentiment. To exhaust oneself in a grand memorial service for the deceased doesn't even come close to a kind word while he is still alive. These days the world is in decline; people are quick to blame others who stray an inch, while they themselves stray a foot and don't notice it. They are so busy

looking over their shoulders they don't see that they them-
selves are unfilial.

> Rare luck it is indeed
> To be born in human form.
> As supple bamboo grows,
> Straight is the road
> That all should follow.

Since Father was unable to sleep after midnight, the
length of the night began to bother him. "Hasn't it started
to grow light yet? Hasn't the cock crowed?" he asked me
three times, four times, seven times, nine times. But the
only answer in the pale starlight was an owl moaning of the
deep night from the shadows cast here and there by the fir
and maple trees next to the eaves. Even though there was
once a case of a man making them open the barrier gates by
imitating a cock's crow, the passage of night is in fact the
work of Heaven. And since I know neither the magical
skill of putting fire in a bag, nor do I have the power to
bring back the setting sun, all I could do was trim the wick
of the lamp and keep vigil over his resting form.

*   *   *

Fifth Month, Eleventh Day

It was time to mind the field, and everyone took up his
scythe and clod breaker and went out. Father and I were
left alone. He was sleeping peacefully, and while I boiled
up his medicine, I sat there watching over him, repeatedly
brushing flies away from his sleeping body. Later he began
to speculate about the future.

"As sick as I am, I am thinking a lot about what is going
to happen after I die. Everyone is this house treats you and

me like enemies. And they malign you. Only as long as I am alive to act as a buffer and protect you can you stay even a short time here. But after I die, what can you do against them? Day after day, night after night, the unbearable torments of hell will not cease. It is as clear as the reflection in a mirror that you will then ignore my last wishes and go wandering off to other places. Yet it is difficult for any living creature to escape the discomfort of sickness, the pain of death. And if you were to return to this village lame and bent with age, the people of this family would most certainly revile, and treat you worse than a cat or dog, saying, "Didn't we tell you so?" And at that, how sad and mortified would I be, even from beyond the grave!" And tears streamed down my father's face.

At this, I, too, burst into tears of gratitude. Surely only a parent could take pity on such a good-for-nothing orphan as I. I couldn't stop my tears, but finally I looked up and said, "Don't dwell on such matters. I'll get you better in next to no time, even if I have to take on your illness myself. Now hurry up and get well. I'll take a wife, just as you want me to. We'll serve you just as you wish." At this, Father smiled with pleasure.

Since it was now noon, people were returning one by one from the fields..

Fifth Month, Twelfth Day

More and more the patient wanted cold water, but since the doctor had strictly proscribed it, I offered him only water that I had boiled. He fretted that the water was warm. It must have been the discomfort of his fever that made him want cold water. Nevertheless, how could I give him something that would be like poison for him? Referring to what the doctor had ordered, Father said, "His advice is heartless indeed," and he would have none of it. Until yesterday my stepmother had been fighting with my father, and now, ignoring the fact that it might be bad for him, she went ahead and offered him three or four cupfuls of well water in a Tenmoku bowl.

"Now *this* is fresh water! The water I was getting before was fake. That's a hell of a thing for Issa to do, tricking me like that!" Father complained. Bi Gan remonstrated with King Zhou and got his heart torn out. When scoundrels are rampant in the state, it is difficult to be humane and righteous.

After that, Father enjoyed drinking water, and each day he had a gallon or so. There I was, in attendance at his bedside, yet unable to dissuade him from doing something harmful right before my eyes. There was just nothing I could do about it. Although they say that good medicine is bitter to the taste, it has a good effect on the patient. And although they say that admonitions are hard on the ears, only thus is a shaky home steadied. Father smiles with pleasure at the person who offers him poison, and thinks ill of the one who forces medicine on him. If his family really wished for his recovery with all their hearts, why should they be giving him things that aren't good for him? Well, one can't always have one's own way in this world....

Fifth Month, Thirteenth Day

"I feel so good this morning that I want some sake," Father said. But since sake was strictly forbidden by the doctor, I decided I couldn't give him even one drop until he recovered. But someone who'd come to visit him said, "If you go this far in stopping him from doing what he likes, you may regret it later if he should die. Your regrets then will be to no avail. It would only be kind to give him one or two mouthfuls of whatever he wants, although only a little."

And those people who were just waiting for any chance to do their mischief pricked up their ears and sat there listening. They said, "This morning why don't you trust the patient's wishes? Give him some sake! Give him some sake!"

So I did. Like a boat that had reached its mooring, father drank as if a long-desired dream had been realized. Like a whale gulping seawater, he downed five *go* during the morning. For a man who had not eaten solid food in twenty days to do such a thing—why, even a three-year-old would frown if he heard about it. I alone wrung my hands, but it was difficult to stand up to the two of them and in the end I did not speak out. How it galled me the way they pretended to be outwardly caring for Father, when in fact they were rejoicing in their hearts at his pending death.

Fifth Month, Fourteenth Day

When I looked at his face this morning, I was not happy to see the swelling, which had not been there yesterday. Fearing that the effects of the alcohol had risen to his face, I checked his entire body, too. The swelling was all over. I wondered if there was a medicine for getting rid of alcohol poisoning, but out here in this backwater, we would never be able to get hold of it in time, and so I was left wondering what to do next. People always want to see what's hidden, to eat what's forbidden, and sure enough, Father declared, "I want some more sake." We fought over my deciding today to disobey his wishes and not give him any sake. Father said angrily, "You are not a doctor—what do you know about this? Yesterday I drank and drank without any harm. What could be so bad about it? Now stop putting me off and get out the sake right now!"

I had quite run out of admonishments, so I said, "Well, if that's the way it is, then just one more cup...." and brought him the sake. He smacked his lips as he drank it. Although he wanted another cup, I urged him to stop with just the one.

A visitor said, "To cut your father off like that...." But sake stoked Father's fever like kindling stoking a fire, and I could not bring myself to do anything that would prolong his illness.

✻   ✻   ✻

Fifth Month, Seventeenth Day

Day after day, the swelling in Father's face continued, and I was also worried about the mucus rattling around in his throat. In the beginning of his illness there had been signs of a bit of mucus building up, but now the mucus and the swelling had become the main worry. Before we had always managed to force the phlegm down with sugar, and until now it had been no great problem. But now I felt it was too uncertain to be left to untrained people, and so I sent a messenger hurrying off with the news to Jinseki in Nojiri. I waited, sure that even now it would be too late, but something must have held Jinseki up and he didn't come all that day. It was the time of the short nights of the fifth month, yet there was not a night through which I did not anxiously await daybreak. But on this night in particular, because the doctor didn't come, the dawn was slow in breaking. Nonetheless, by breakfast Father had settled down somewhat.

Fifth Month, Eighteenth Day

By daybreak Father seemed to be feeling better, and I was pleased when he said he would like to sit up and lean on something. When I piled the bedclothes up as usual, he sat propped up on them for a short while; but then his breathing began to get difficult, and he said that he wanted to lie back down again. As this was going on, Jinseki arrived and immediately examined Father. He reported, "His pulse is fine, and but for the swelling and the mucus. . . . I'll give him some medicine to reduce the swelling."

He took a spoon, quickly made up the medicine, boiled it, and gave it to Father. Perhaps as a result, Father urinated a number of times. His condition seemed to improve and he slept peacefully.

While I was sitting there as usual, rubbing his feet, Father suddenly opened his eyes and said, "You have been so good about taking care of me these long days and nights. It is because of the strong ties between father and son that you happened along at this time. I hope you don't consider the relationship a burden." He spoke with much feeling.

I replied, "It is only because of the parents' kindness that anyone has a life at all. So even if someone's parents were sick like this for ten years or twenty years, how could he be negligent? Just stop worrying about it and get better!"

Father answered, "I, too, would like to recover, but since this is the most serious illness I've had in my life, it's hard to tell whether or not this may be the end. Should I die, do just as I say: take a wife, and don't move far away from this area. Do not disobey me in this after I've gone."

"Such kind words! As the gods are my witness, my heart is not wood or stone, so how could I let you down even after your death? Don't worry about it at all." As I spoke soothingly to him, he began to sleep peacefully. Night fell, refreshing.

It was still dark, about four in the morning, and as there was someone going to Zenkōji, Father said, "While you're at it, I'd like some sugar."

At this, my stepmother grew visibly upset, and calculating the amount of sugar he'd had up until now, she said, "So you think you want to have more sugar.... It's just wasted on someone who's about to die." And she railed on about this and that. Since Father had told me to also eat the sugar that was used in preparing the medication for his mucus, she suspected that I was taking it, and she berated me about it. Any way you look at it, it's a terribly greedy world.... We didn't get any sugar for Father after all.

Earlier that night, after about midnight, his fever had risen quite high and Father had said he wanted some cold water. As I was about to go out and draw the water from the well, he cautioned me as though he thought I was his little boy again, saying, "Don't fall in the well!"

My stepmother had been sleeping, but she'd heard this. She suddenly said with harsh indignation, "Your treasured son! So you love him as much as this?" Her wrath was aroused and her hair stood on end like needles as she glared at us fiercely. Surely this must have been what the great serpent looked like.

Fifth Month, Nineteenth Day

Until now Father had been smiling and in good spirits in the mornings. But this morning he didn't even care for warm water, and the dull coloring of his face did not give me much hope. After noon his illness took a turn for the worse. He was no longer writhing, no longer saying, "Rub this spot! Pat that spot!" He just fell into a peaceful sleep like a wooden Buddha that had been knocked over on its side.

Someone remarked, "They say that when the illness spirits have fled, the patient usually sleeps without eating for three or four days, so this is not a bad sign."

My only wish was for Father to recover quickly, and so it made me happy to hear that there had been cases like this before. I started feeling that all my nursing was paying off and I could relax.

About four in the morning, everyone was sleeping peacefully and things were quiet. I, too, was at last lying down, half asleep and half awake from the exhaustion of these many days. Father opened his eyes and said, "I'm g-g-g-going... Please walk along with me."

When I asked him where he was going, he chanted in a voice that rang out as though he were no longer sick, "It goes without saying, 'With unwavering, devoted heart, I long to be reborn in that land.'"

In my heart I thought what he had said was inauspicious, but I calmed myself and decided that it must have been delirious talk.

He said, over and over again, "Hey! Let's go! Let's go!" and so I made as if I were going to try to help him up. When he said, "Hey, let's go!" I, too, said, "Let's go!" After I had said this as many as nine times, he fell back into a peaceful sleep.

When I thought about it afterward, I realized that these were the last words he spoke. They were his death poem.

Fifth Month, Twentieth Day

Father's fever was gradually rising. In the morning he ate only a little bit of *awako;* from around noon, his face was ghastly pale, his eyes swollen and half-shut, and he moved his lips as though he wanted to say something. With each inhalation and exhalation, his life was being sucked away in the rattling of the mucus. His breathing was getting progressively weaker. Through the window entered the light of the sun as it moved toward its end like a lamb to the slaughter. Father could no longer distinguish people's faces. There seemed to be no hope left.

Oh the pain of it! Would that I could have exchanged my life for his and just once more have seen him healthy again. When he had said he wanted something to eat, I had prohibited it, telling him it would be bad for him. Now I felt that all the resources of Jivaka or Bian Que would not be enough, that the power of all the gods would not suffice, and that there was nothing else to do but recite the *nembutsu.*

> His sleeping form—
> I shoo away the flies today.
> There's nothing more to do.

As the day drew to a close, I vainly tried to wet his lips with water from a vessel by his bedside. The twentieth-night moon shone in through the window, and all the neighborhood was sleeping quietly. As a cock's crow in the distance could be heard announcing the dawn, Father's breathing became increasingly shallow, and the mucus that I'd been concerned about from the very beginning was now time and again blocking his throat. If the thread of his life was to be cut away, I wanted at least to remove the mucus. But I was not Hua Tuo and so did not know any of his skillful techniques. Dejected, I threw up my hands in despair. The suffering, the grief in my heart as I could do nothing but wait for his final moments. . . . Even the gods showed no mercy. the night moved brightly into dawn, and about six o'clock, as though he had fallen into a deep sleep, Father breathed his last.

I took hold of his empty, pitiful body. Would that this was all a dream from which I would awake! But dream or reality, I felt I was wandering in darkness without a lamp, on this cold dawn in this fleeting world.

The impermanent spring flowers are seduced and scattered by the wind; this ignorant world's autumn moon is surrounded and hidden by clouds. The world knows— need I repeat it?—"That what lives must perish; that which is joined together will certainly fall apart." And although this is the road that all must travel eventually, I was foolish enough not to believe that my own father could go as soon as yesterday or today.

Those people who only yesterday defied my father and quarreled with him, now are clinging to his corpse, tears streaming down their faces. Amid the clouds of their repetitions of Amida's name, I realized that the eternal vows of husband and wife—to grow old together, to be buried together—were in fact ever binding.

＊　　＊　　＊

Fifth Month, Twenty-third Day

Dawn. . . . It was time for us to gather up Father's ashes. Each of us picked up a pair of hollow chopsticks and walked to Adashi moor. Even the last traces of smoke had disappeared this morning, and there was only the sound of the wind blowing uneasily in the pines. When I had come back on that night in the third month, I had received the joyful cup of wine. Now, at dawn, I was gathering up the sad white bones of parting. The world is like a rope, plaited

214   *The Essential Haiku*

with strands of joy and anger, pain and pleasure. All that meets will part. This present state of affairs should not surprise me, but until now I had always relied on Father whenever I returned to my village. From now on, whose strength could I depend on? I have no wife or child to hold my affection. I haven't a thing to my name and am drifting like foam on the water, blowing along with the wind like a speck of dust. Yet this string of beads that is my life is difficult to snap.

> Left behind
> and drenched as the grass,
> with drops of dew.

Around midday people gathered to lend a hand or to talk, and for a while I seemed to forget my sadness. But by evening nearly everyone had gone home, and by the light of the lamp the place where Father's sickbed had been filled me with sad longings. For a moment I had the sensation that I was waiting there again for Father to waken from his sleep. I kept seeing his body racked with suffering. The sound of his voice calling to me remained in my ears. When I dozed off, I saw him in my dreams. When I awoke, his image loomed before my eyes.

> Night after night
> how he was plagued
> by fleas and mosquitoes!

We cannot make water flow back again, we cannot return fire to the flint. No matter how many regrets we may have, they are all useless. Each of the relatives on whom we think we can rely will pass on to decay. Ah, this lonely orphan Issa, abandoned like someone banished to an unknown land! How piteous I felt.

Fifth Month, Twenty-eighth Day

It was the seventh day after Father's death. While he was still alive, he'd told people that he wanted me to get married and settle down here. He'd even given me those instructions directly. But there were some people among those to whom Father had spoken who pretended they never heard him say such a thing. They were so deeply mired in the Six Passions that they are not likely to obey Father's last wishes. And since I am not willing to face their red-faced anger, perhaps I should go back to my old life as a wanderer and hide myself away in some cramped cave or wooden shelter. As long as I am protected from the wind and sheltered from the rain, what shame is there in leading such a penniless existence. But to give up and go away without a word would be disobeying my father's wishes. Not even a rough stone can produce a spark unless it is struck; even a cracked bell will ring when you hit it. This is the natural way of heaven and earth. I would be disobeying my dead father if I rashly left the village without waiting for a response. I consulted the others about my inheritance and found that they intended to honor Father's last requests. Thereupon I decided to follow the instructions of the family and pursued the matter no further that day.

> With my father
> I would look out at dawn
> over green fields.

FROM *A YEAR OF MY LIFE*

(1819)

Prose Translation by
NOBUYUKI YUASA

1

My little daughter was born just last May, but I give her a grown-up's portion of rice cake for her New Year's breakfast—

> Crawl, laugh,
> do what you want,
> you're two today!

First of January, in the second year of Bunsei.

I have no servant to draw the first water of the New Year:

> In my stead—
> a crow's cold bath
> in the first water of the year.

A lake in spring:

> Spring moon—
> even a turtle
> can tell the season.

In front of Zenkōji Temple on a festival day:

> The buds of the willow—
> gray as an ash-gray cat—
> are also votive flowers.

*   *   *

One balmy day in March a young priest named Takamaru from Myōsenji Temple—a mere boy of eleven—set out with a strapping priest named Kanryō for Araizaka to pick spring herbs and flowers. Now it happened that Takamaru slipped while crossing a bridge and fell into the waters of a raging river that was fed by freshets of melting snow from Mount Iizuna. Kanryō heard the boy's scream and rushed to help—but all his efforts proved vain. At first he could see Takamaru's head rising above the water, and then a hand. But Takamaru's cries grew fainter, till soon his voice sounded no louder than the shrilling of summer mosquitoes. Alas! The young priest disappeared in the swirling torrent and left nothing but his image—stamped on the eyes of Kanryō. Later, the people searched up and down the river for Takamaru with lighted torches. At last they found him—wedged between two rocks. But it was too late. He was dead, and there was none who could bring him back to life again. Even the sleeves of those unused to weeping were wet with tears when they discovered in his pocket a few blossoms of butterbur—just picked—

perchance intended as a happy present for his parents had it not been for his untimely death. They carried him home on a litter, a little past eight in the evening. His parents ran up to the body and wept bitterly, in full view of all the world. It is true that they were priests and used to preach indifference to life's vicissitudes. But who can blame them? It is only human that their strong affection for their child should loose the knots that bound their heartstrings when they beheld him so untimely dead. This boy had been alive and fresh when he left home that morning. And now it was evening, and he lay still and dead. His body was cremated two days later. As I went to join the procession, I wrote:

> I never thought
> to turn the buds
> of spring to smoke,
> to see it rising
> as it rises now.

Surely the flowers, too—no less than Takamaru's parents —must weep to be cut down and cast into the flames in the course of a single day, just as they are lifting their faces to the spring after a long winter's snow. For flowers, too, have life, and will not they, as we, pass to Nirvana in the end?

Silent meditation:

> A huge frog and I
> staring at each other,
> neither of us moves.

> Moonlight on the plum,
> what is it?
> Am I supposed to steal a blossom?

Above the dark corners
of Matsushima,
       a skylark singing.

The big cat
frisks its tail,
       toying with the butterfly.

March 7, a festival day in Hoshina village:

Beneath the falling blossoms
no shrine
       but gets its offering.

The willow yields
to let me pass
       beyond the hedge.

Stuffed with rice cake—
for digestion's sake,
       I'll go out and graft my tree.

       3

It was widely rumored that certain persons had heard ce-
lestial music coming down from heaven around two
o'clock in the morning on New Year's Day. And they say
it has been heard every eighth night since. Some told me in
all seriousness that they actually heard the music at such
and such a place on such and such a night. Others dis-
missed it as simply a prank played by the wanton wind. I,
for one, was inclined to take the idea seriously, but could
neither accept it as completely true or reject it as absolutely
impossible. For heaven and earth are filled with strange

and mysterious powers, and we have all heard of the dancing maidens, and the "sweet dew" that came from above. Is it not possible that the courtiers in the halls of heaven may have been rejoicing to see the world at peace and called for music—and if we could not hear it, is it not probable that it was our sinful natures that prevented us? In any event, I found myself intrigued, and invited a group of my friends to come to my humble cottage on the nineteenth day of March. We all listened intently, from early evening on, but we heard nothing until the first sunbeams touched the far end of the eastern sky. Then all at once we heard a voice—we heard music—coming from the plum tree near my window.

> Only birds
> sing the music of heaven
> in this world.

*   *   *

5

It was rumored abroad that an exceedingly beautiful crop of peonies had come into bloom at my friend Nabuchi's house, and that many people for miles around had come to look at them. Accordingly, I dropped in one day to see them for myself. The flower bed was more than fifteen feet long, and laid out beneath an elaborate canopy. It was crowded with full-blown peonies, packed in side by side— white peonies and red peonies, and peonies of purple and other colors. Among them one black and one yellow especially caught my attention because of their unusual colors. When I looked once more, however, and scrutinized them more carefully, I noticed they seemed rather dry, and compared with the healthy young peonies all around them, they looked like mere painted carcasses. They were, of course, the handiwork of my friend. He had made them out of paper and tied them under the leaves of the true peonies as a joke on his guests. His witty deception greatly tickled me. And he certainly was guilty of no wrong. He charged no one a penny for coming to see his flowers. On the contrary, he provided all who came with generous quantities of wine and tea.

> Hidden in the leaves
>   even scraps of paper
>   have the faces of peonies.

*   *   *

6

The children of this province play a strange game. They take a live frog and bury him, and cover his grave with leaves of plantain grass, singing the following song as they work.

> Hey ho! The frog is dead!
> Hey ho! The frog is dead.
> Come, let us bury him,
> Come, let us bury him,
> Under plantain leaves!
> Under plantain leaves!

In *Honsō-Kōmoku*, a Chinese treatise on plants, we find that plantain grass is called "frog's skin," whereas in the dialect of this province, it is called "frog's leaf." The correspondence between the Chinese and Japanese popular names can hardly be a coincidence. There must have been some special meaning in this children's game when it was first created years ago.

*   *   *

There once lived a physician named Nakamura in the town of Suzaka in the province of Shinano. One day, just for the fun of it, he killed a pair of snakes while they were coupling. That night he was seized by a sharp pain in his loins and died. His son, Santetsu, who was a very stout man, likewise became a physician. But on the night of his marriage he found that he was sexually impotent. In exasperation he tried himself with many other women, but always with the same result. I hear that despair has finally driven him to live in complete isolation.

Up to the time when I became aware of this case, I had never allowed myself to take such horror stories seriously. I had always imagined they were the peculiar province of a certain kind of storybook, such as the *Uji Shūi Monogatari* and others of that stripe. But considering it more deeply, it now seemed all too probable that it was truly the spiteful vengeance of the snakes that had undone this family and caused it so much pain.

All creatures, not excluding even fleas and lice, are endowed with life. It is just as dear to one as to another, and it is a grave sin to kill any living thing, particularly in the act of procreation.

> Not knowing
> it's a tub they're in,
> the fish cooling at the gate.

Quick, into the mist,
little bird,
   you're free!

   Lying still as a Buddha,
I let a late mosquito
   suck my blood

                              OEMARU

A carp dying in a tub
Spends his last moments
Lashing the water with his fins,
So man wastes his little life
In senseless agitation.

                        LORD MITSUTOSHI

Minnows are helpless
Caught in the branches of a tree
Set out to lure them,
So we too are tangled
In the snare of ignorance.

                        LORD TOSHIYORI

   The toll collectors
keep burning wormwood
   as the plums blossom.

   Hearing a voice
the doe takes up her stand
   beside the fawn.

A lotus stem,
slightly bent—
in this world.

* * * *

11

There was once a very cruel woman who lived in the village of Tasuta in the province of Yamato. And she refused to feed her stepchild for ten consecutive days. When the child was about to die of hunger, she showed him a bowl of rice and said, "Take this, and offer it to the stone statue beside the road. If he eats it, you can have some too." There was nothing the poor child could do. he had to obey. But as he sat down to pray before the stone image, a great miracle happened. The stone statue opened his gigantic mouth and devoured the rice as greedily as if he himself had been a starving child. After that, they say, the horns of cruelty dropped from the woman's brow, and she ceased discriminating between the stepchild and her own children. And if, perchance, you should ever pay a visit to this village, you can still see that stone statue, standing where it was, and you will never fail to see offerings laid before it.

12

Last summer, when the day for setting out bamboo slips was drawing nigh, a child was born to us. We named her Sato, hoping she might grow in wisdom, despite the fact that she was born in ignorance. This year, when her birthday came round, she bobbed her head at us, and waved her hands, and cried, which was her way of telling us that she wanted a paper windmill of a kind that was very popular among the small children. So we bought her one. But she soon set to licking it and sucking it, and finally with prodigal indifference, she flung it away. Her mind seems to flit from one thing to another, resting nowhere. Now she is busy with a clay pot, but soon she smashes it. Next she will be fascinated by a paper screen, but she soon tears it. And if we praise her for her actions, she accepts our approval at face value, and smiles delightedly. Not a cloud crosses over her sunny mind. She is pure moonlight, and beams all over from head to foot, delighting us more than the most accomplished performer on the stage could possibly do. Occasionally a visitor will ask her to point out a dog or a bird to him, and at such times she is completely captivating—from the tip of her toes to the top of her little head. She seems just like a butterfly, poised lightly on a spring of young spring grass, resting her wings.

I believe this child lives in a special state of grace, and enjoys divine protection from Buddha. For when the evening comes when once a year we hold a memorial service for the dead, and I have lit the candles on the family altar and rung the bell for prayer, she crawls out swiftly, wherever she may be, and softly folds her hands, like little bracken sprouts, and says her prayers in such a sweet, small voice—in such a lovely way. For myself, I am old enough that my hair is touched with frost, and every year adds another wave of wrinkles to my brow, yet so far I have not found grace with Buddha, and waste my days and months in meaningless activity. I am ashamed to think my child, who is only two years old, is closer to the truth than I. And yet no sooner do I leave the altar than I sow the seeds of future torments, hating the flies that crawl across my knee, killing the mosquitoes that swarm around the table, and even worse, drinking the wine that Buddha has prohibited.

Just as I was reproaching myself in this fashion, the moonlight touched our gate, adding a breath of coolness to the evening air. A group of children dancing outside suddenly lifted their voices and cried aloud. My little girl at once threw down the bowl she had been playing with, and crawled out to the porch, where she too cried out and stretched forth her hands to the moon. Watching her, I quite forgot my old age and my sinful nature, and indulged myself with reflections that when she should be old enough to boast long hair with waving curls, we might let her dance, and that would be more beautiful, I fancied, than to hear the music of twenty-five dancing maidens.

⁎   ⁎   ⁎

14

It is a commonplace of life that the greatest pleasure issues ultimately in the greatest grief. Yet why—why is it that this child of mine, who has not tasted half the pleasures that the world has to offer, who ought, by rights, to be as fresh and green as the vigorous young needles of the everlasting pine—why must she lie here on her deathbed, swollen with blisters, caught in the loathsome clutches of the vile god of smallpox. Being, as I am, her father, I can scarcely bear to watch her withering away—a little more each day—like some pure, untainted blossom that is ravished by the sudden onslaught of mud and rain.

After two or three days, however, her blisters dried up and the scabs began to fall away—like a hard crust of dirt that has been softened by melting snow. In our joy we made what we call a "priest in a straw robe." We poured hot wine ceremoniously over his body, and packed him and the god of smallpox off together. Yet our hopes proved to be vain. She grew weaker and weaker and finally, on the twenty-first of June, as the morning glories were just closing their flowers, she closed her eyes forever. Her mother embraced the cold body and cried bitterly. For myself, I knew well it was no use to cry, that water once flown past the bridge does not return, and blossoms that are scattered are gone beyond recall. Yet try as I would, I could not, simply could not, cut the binding cord of human love.

> The world of dew
> is the world of dew.
> And yet, and yet—

*   *   *

15

Not far from the village of Shiba someone caught a baby crow—no bigger than a lump of coal—and put it in a cage in front of the house. That night I heard the mother flying back and forth above the house, crying over and over again in the darkness.

> Over and over
> the she-crow's voice
> crying in the dark.

*   *   *

There is a proverb that says, "If you seek shelter, then rest your wings beneath the largest tree." And indeed there are always some who are willing to kneel down before the wealthy or to oil their tongues in the presence of the powerful.

Here in this village is a large chestnut tree that stands near Suwa Shrine. And although the tree does not seem particularly heavy-laden, not a person comes by who cannot pick up a chestnut or two every morning.

IV

BASHŌ ON
POETRY

LEARN FROM THE PINE

Learn about pines from the pine, and about bamboo from the bamboo.

Don't follow in the footsteps of the old poets, seek what they sought.

The basis of art is change in the universe. What's still has changeless form. Moving things change, and because we cannot put a stop to time, it continues unarrested. To stop a thing would be to halve a sight or sound in our heart. Cherry blossoms whirl, leaves fall, and the wind flits them both along the ground. We cannot arrest with our eyes or ears what lies in such things. Were we to gain mastery over them, we would find that the life of each thing had vanished without a trace.

Make the universe your companion, always bearing in mind the true nature of things—mountains and rivers, trees and grasses, and humanity—and enjoy the falling blossoms and the scattering leaves.

One should know that a hokku is made by combining things.

The secret of poetry lies in treading the middle path between the reality and the vacuity of the world.

One must first of all concentrate one's thoughts on an object. Once one's mind achieves a state of concentration and the space between oneself and the object has disappeared, the essential nature of the object can be perceived. Then express it immediately. If one ponders it, it will vanish from the mind.

Sabi is the color of the poem. It does not necessarily refer to the poem that describes a lonely scene. If a man goes to war wearing stout armor or to a party dressed up in gay clothes, and if this man happens to be an old man, there is something lonely about him. *Sabi* is something like that.

When you are composing a verse, let there not be a hair's breadth separating your mind from what you write. Quickly say what is in your mind; never hesitate a moment.

Composition must occur in an instant, like a woodcutter felling a huge tree, or a swordsman leaping at his enemy. It is also like cutting a ripe watermelon with a sharp knife or like taking a large bite at a pear.

Is there any good in saying everything?

In composing hokku, there are two ways: becoming and making. When a poet who has always been assiduous in pursuit of his aim applies himself to an external object, the color of his mind naturally becomes a poem. In the case of the poet who has not done so, nothing in him will become a poem; he consequently makes the poem through an act of personal will.

Haikai exists only while it's on the writing desk. Once it's taken off, it should be regarded as a mere scrap of paper.

There are three elements in *haikai*. Its feeling can be called loneliness *(sabi)*. This plays with refined dishes, but contents itself with humble fare. Its total effect can be called elegance. This lives in figured silks and embroidered brocades, but does not forget a person clad in woven straw. Its language can be called aesthetic madness. Language resides in untruth and ought to comport with truth. It is difficult to reside in truth and sport with untruth. These three elements do not exalt a humble person to heights. They put an exalted person in a low place.

The profit of *haikai* lies in making common speech right.

If you describe a green willow in the spring rain it will be excellent as a *renga* verse. *Haikai*, however, needs more homely images, such as a crow picking mud snails in a rice paddy.

The hokku has changed repeatedly since the distant past, but there have only been three changes in the *haikai* link. In the distant past, poets valued lexical links. In the more recent past, poets have stressed content links. Today it is best to link by reflection *(utsuri)*, reverberation *(hibiki)*, scent *(nioi)*, or status *(kurai)*.

In this mortal frame of mine, which is made of a hundred bones and nine orifices, there is something, and this something can be called, for lack of a better name, a windswept spirit, for it is much like thin drapery that is torn and swept away by the slightest stirring of the wind. This something in me took to writing poetry years ago, merely to amuse itself at first, but finally making it its lifelong business. It must be admitted, however, that there were times when it sank into such dejection that it was almost ready to drop its pursuit, or again times when it was so puffed up with pride that it exulted in vain victories over others. Indeed, ever since it began to write poetry, it has never found peace with itself, always wavering between doubts of one kind or another. At one time it wanted to gain security by entering the service of a court, or at another it wished to measure the depth of its ignorance by trying to be a scholar, but it was prevented from either by its unquenchable love of poetry. The fact is, it knows no other art than the art of writing poetry, and therefore it hangs on to it more or less blindly.

Poetry is a fireplace in summer or a fan in winter.

After wandering from place to place I returned to Edo and spent the winter at a district called Tachibana, where I am still, though it is already the second month of the new year. During this time I tried to give up poetry and remain silent, but every time I did so a poetic sentiment would solicit my heart and something would flicker in my mind. Such is the magic spell of poetry. Because of it, I abandoned everything and left home; almost penniless, I have kept myself by going around begging. How invincible is the power of poetry to reduce me to a tattered beggar.

There is a common element permeating Saigyō's lyric poetry, Sōgi's linked verse, Sesshu's painting, and Rikyu's tea ceremony. It is the poetic spirit (*fūrabo*), the spirit that leads one to follow nature and become a friend with things of the seasons. For a person who has the spirit, everything he sees becomes a flower, and everything he imagines turns into a moon. Those who do not see the flower are no different from barbarians, and those who do not imagine the moon are akin to beasts. Leave barbarians and beasts behind; follow nature and return to nature.

Every form of insentient existence—plants, stones, or utensils—has its individual feelings similar to those of men.

When we observe calmly, we discover that all things have their fulfillment.

One need not be a *haikai* poet, but if someone doesn't live inside ordinary life and understand ordinary feelings, he's not likely to be a poet.

Clad in a black robe, I was neither a priest nor an ordinary man, for I wandered ceaselessly, like a bat that passes for a bird at one time and a mouse at another.

I always feel when sitting in company with Kikaku at the same party that he is anxious to compose a verse that will please the whole company. I have no such intention.

It's admirable to have an undistracted mind, praiseworthy to be without worldly talent and knowledge. The same can be said of a homeless wanderer, but leading a life so liberated requires an iron will.

Since ancient times, those with a feeling for poetry did not mind carrying knapsacks on their backs or putting straw sandals on their feet or wearing simple hats that barely protected them from the elements. They took delight in disciplining their minds through hardship and thereby attaining a knowledge of the true nature of things.

One needs to work to achieve enlightenment and then return to the common world.

The bones of *haikai* are plainness and oddness.

A verse that has something interesting in it is all right, even if its meaning isn't very clear.

Eat vegetable soup rather than duck stew.

The style I have in mind is a light one both in form and in structure, like the impression of looking at the sandy bed of a shallow river.

The leaves of the *bashō* tree are large enough to cover a lute. When they flutter in the wind, they remind me of the injured tail of a phoenix, and when they are torn, they remind me of a dragon's ears. The tree does bear flowers, but unlike other flowers there is nothing gay about them. The big trunk of the tree is untouched by the ax, for it is utterly useless to build with. The monk Huai-su wrote on the leaves, and Chang Heng-ch'u saw the new leaves unfurling and took incentive in *hsi* studies. I love the tree, however, for its very uselessness. I take my ease in its shade and am fond of it because it is so easily torn by wind and rain.

FROM KYORAI'S
CONVERSATIONS WITH
BASHŌ

Translation by
DONALD KEENE

Yuku haru wo	The departing spring
Ōmi no hito to	With the men of Ōmi
Oshimikeru	Have I lamented.

BASHŌ

The Master said, "Shōhaku criticized this poem on the grounds that I might just as well have said 'Tamba' instead of 'Ōmi' or 'departing year' instead of departing spring.' How does this criticism strike you?" Kyorai replied, "Shōhaku's criticism misses the mark entirely. What could be more natural than to regret the passing of the spring, when the waters of the Lake of Ōmi are veiled so enchantingly in mist? Besides, it is especially fitting a poem for one who lives by the lake to have written." The Master said, "Yes, the poets of old loved spring in this province almost as much as the capital." Kyorai, deeply struck by these words, continued. "If you were in Ōmi at the close of the year, why should you regret its passing? Or, if you were in Tamba at the end of the spring, you would not be likely to have such a feeling. What truth there is in the feelings of a man who has genuinely been stirred by some sight of Nature!" The Master said, "Kyorai, you are a person with whom I can talk about poetry." He was very pleased.

✳   ✳   ✳

Kogarishi ni
Futsuka no tsuki no
Fukichiru ka

Will the two-day moon
Be blown from the sky
By the winter wind?

KAKEI

Kogarashi no
Chi ni mo otosanu
Shigure ka na

Kept by the winter wind
From falling to earth—
The drizzling rain.

KYORAI

Kyorai said, "I feel that Kakei's verse is far superior to mine. By asking if it will be 'blown from the sky' he makes his mention of the two-day moon all the more clever." Bashō answered, "Kakei's verse is built; around the words 'two-day moon.' Take away the 'two-day moon' and there is nothing left to the poem. It is not apparent on what you based your poem. It is good all around."

✳   ✳   ✳

Kiyotaki ya	Clear cascades!
Nami ni chiri naki	In the immaculate waves
Natsu no tsuki	The summer moon.

BASHŌ

One day when the Master was lying on his sickbed in Osaka, he called Kyorai to him and said, "This verse resembles one I composed not long ago at Sonome's house:

Shiragiku no	The white chrysanthemum
Me ni tatete miru	Even when lifted to the eye
Chiri mo nashi	Remains immaculate.

BASHŌ

I have therefore changed the 'Clear cascades' verse to:

Kiyotaki ya	Clear cascades!
Nami ni chirikomu	Into the waves scatter
Aomatsuba	Blue pine needles.

BASHŌ

"The rough draft of the original poem must be in Yameï's house. Please destroy it." But it was too late—the poem had already appeared in several collections.

This example demonstrates what pains Bashō took with every verse, master though he was.

*   *   *

Omakaji ya
Akashi no tomari
Hototogisu

Port the helm!
There, by Akashi Harbor,
A skylark!

KAKEI

This poem was being considered for inclusion in *The Monkey's Cloak*. Kyorai said, "It is just like the Master's:

No wo yoko ni
Uma hikimuke yo
Hotogisu

Across the fields
Turn the horse's head—
A skylark!

"It should not be included." The Master said, "The 'skylark of Akashi' is not a bad image." Kyorai replied. "I don't know about the 'skylark of Akashi,' but the poem merely substitutes a boat for a horse. It shows no originality." The Master commented, "He hasn't made any advance in the conception of the verse, but you may include it or not as you please on the basis of the Akashi skylark." We finally did not include it.

*   *   *

Kyorai's poem below has been interpreted as referring to himself, older but less talented than most of Bashō's pupils—"a back number."

Furumai ya
Shimoza ni naoru

Kozo no hina

The attitudes they strike!
I straighten on the lower
  shelf
Last year's dolls.

KYORAI

Kyorai wrote this verse because of the special meaning it had for him. For the first line he had first tried "the old court cap" or else "the paper cloak," but they left nothing to the imagination, and mentioning the doll's costume obscured his underlying thought. On the other hand, an expression like "how pitiable!" or "how unfortunate!" was too feeble. When, having finally hit on the present opening line, Kyorai asked the Master about it, he replied, "If you really insist on putting your heart into the first line, you ought to say something like Shintoku's 'Ah, the world of men!' Your 'attitudes they strike' is not quite right, but it will do."

*   *   *

Ta no heri no	Along the border of the fields
Mame tsutai yuku	Following the bean plants
Hotaru ka na	Go the fireflies.
	BANKO

This verse was originally one by Bonchō that the Master had corrected. When we were compiling *The Monkey's Cloak*, Bonchō remarked, "This verse has nothing special to recommend it. Let's leave it out." Kyorai answered, "The lights of the fireflies following the bean plants at the edge of a field splendidly evoke a dark night." But Bonchō was not convinced by these words. The Master said, "If Bonchō throws it away, I'll pick it up. It fortunately happens that one of the Iga poets has a similar verse that I can modify into this one." Thus it finally appeared as Banko's poem.

                    *   *   *

Kiraretaru   Stabbed to death!
Yume wa makoto ka   Was my dream true?
Nomi no ato   The marks of a flea.

                                    KIKAKU

Kyorai said, "Kikaku is really a clever writer. Who else
would ever have thought of writing a poem about merely
being bitten by a flea?" The Master said, "You're quite
right. He's the Prince Teika of the haiku. He deals with tri-
fling matters in a most grandiloquent way." This criticism
seemed to me to describe Kikaku's art completely.

                    *   *   *

Ototoi wa   The day before yesterday
Ano yama koetsu   I crossed the mountain
                               over there—
Hanazakari   With the full bloom of the
                               cherry.

                                    KYORAI

Kyorai wrote this verse two or three years before *The
Monkey's Cloak* was compiled. At the time the Master said
to him, "I doubt whether anyone will appreciate this verse
now. You'll have to wait a year or two." Later he wrote
Kyorai on his journey with Tokoku to Yoshino, "My
mind has been so dominated now by one poem about the
cherry blossoms of Yoshino and now by another, each of

---

which so completely describes the scene, that I myself have not written a single verse at Yoshino. All I do every day as I go along is to recite your 'The day before yesterday I crossed the mountain over there.'" The poem was acclaimed when Kyorai later read it to other people. How did the Master know that it would be popular in a year or two? Kyorai, for one, never dreamt it.

*   *   *

Yamu kari no	A sick wild duck
Yosamu ni ochite	Falling in the evening cold—
Tabine ka na	These traveler's lodgings!

BASHŌ

Ama no ya wa	The fisherman's hut—
Koebi ni majiru	Mixed with little shrimps
Itodo ka na	Some crickets!

BASHŌ

When we were compiling *The Monkey's Cloak* we were asked to choose one of these two poems for inclusion. Bonchō said, "The verse about the sick wild duck is good, but the other about the crickets mixing with the little shrimps has a freshness that makes it truly outstanding." Kyorai said, "The verse about the shrimps is unusual, but had I thought of the scene in the fisherman's hut I could have written it myself. The one about the wild duck, on the other hand, is so noble in tone, so subtly perceptive, that I wonder how anyone could have conceived it." After some discussion we finally asked permission to include both verses. The Master said, laughing, "You seem to have argued yourself into thinking that a sick duck and a little shrimp have about equal value."

*   *   *

Iwahana ya
Koko ni mo hitori
Tsuki no kyaku

The tips of the crags—
Here too is someone,
Guest of the moon.

KYORAI

Kyorai said, "Shadō thinks that the last line should be 'monkey of the moon,' but I think that 'guest' is better." The Master said, "How can he suggest such a word as 'monkey'? What had you in mind when you wrote the poem?" Kyorai answered, "One night, when I was walking in the mountains by the light of the harvest moon, composing poetry as I went along, I noticed another poet standing by the crags." The Master said, "How much more interesting a poem it would be if by the lines 'here too is someone, guest of the moon' you meant yourself. You must be the subject of this verse."

*   *   *

Shimokyō was a very quiet district of Kyoto.

Shimokyō ya
Yuki tsumu ue no
Yo no ame

Shimokyō!
On the piled-up snow
The night rain.

BONCHŌ

This verse at first lacked an opening line, and everyone from the Master downward tried to think of one. At length the Master settled on the above line. Bonchō said yes to it, but still didn't seem satisfied. The Master said, "Bonchō, why don't you think of a better opening line? If you do, I'll never write another haiku!" Kyorai said, "Anyone can see how good a line it is, but it's not so easy to appreciate that no other line would do. If members of some other school of poetry heard what you said, they would think that you were ridiculously self-assured, and they would make up any number of opening lines. But the ones that they considered to be good would seem laughably bad to us."

*   *   *

Inoshishi no   Is that the path
Ne ni yuku kata ya   The wild boar travels to
                     his lair?
Ake no tsuki   The moon at dawning.

KYORAI

When Kyorai asked the Master what he thought of this verse he pondered for a long time without saying whether it was good or bad. Kyorai mistakenly thought that, master though he was, he didn't know how hunters wait at night for a boar to return to his lair at dawn, and explained it all to him in great detail. Then the Master remarked, "The interest of that sight was familiar to the poets of former times. That is why we have the *waka*:

Akenu to te	Now that it has dawned
Nobe yori yama ni	A wind from the clover
Iru shika no	Wafts away the spoor
Ato fukiokuru	Of the deer returning
Ogi no uwakaze	From the fields to their
	mountains.

"When a subject can be treated even within the elegant framework of the *waka,* there does not seem to be much point in giving within the freer compass of the haiku so prosaic a description. The reason that I stopped to think for a while was that the verse seemed somehow interesting, and I was wondering if something couldn't be done with it. But I fear it's hopeless."

*   *   *

Yusuzumi	The evening cool—
Senki okoshite	I got lumbago
Kaerikeri	And went back home.

KYORAI

When Kyorai was first studying *haikai* he asked the Master how to write an opening verse. He replied, "It must be written firmly and clearly." As a test of his abilities Kyorai composed the above verse. When he asked the Master's opinion of it, the Master gave a great laugh and said, "You still haven't got the idea."

*   *   *

Ume ni suzume no	In the plum tree the swallows
Eda no hyaku nari	Form countless clusters on the branches.
	KYORAI

This was a "second verse" composed at the New Year. The Master heard it while he was at his retreat in Fukagawa. He commented, "Plum blossoms are a sight of the second month. Kyorai, how ever did you make the mistake of using that image in a New Year's poem?"

*   *   *

Detchi ga ninau	The water the apprentice
Mizu koboshikeri	Was carrying spilled over.
	BONCHŌ

At first he used the term "night soil." Bonchō asked, "Is it permissible to mention urine and night soil in a poem?" The Master said, "You need not avoid mentioning them. You should not do so more than twice in a hundred verses, and it is quite all right if they aren't mentioned at all." Bonchō changed it to "water."

*   *   *

Tsuma yobu kiji no	The pheasant calling his mate
Mi wo hoso suru	Draws in his body.
	KYORAI

At first it was "The pheasant calling his mate confusedly cries." The Master said, "Kyorai, don't you know even that much about poetry? A poem should have shape. If you say the same thing in the way I suggest your poem will have shape."

*   *   *

Bashō's technique in linked verse demonstrated.

Kuromite takaki   Somber and tall
Kashi no ki no mori   The forest of oaks

Saka hana ni   In and out
Chiisaki mon wo   Through the little gate
Detsu iritsu   To the cherry blossoms.

BASHŌ

When the former verse was given, Kyorai thought how difficult it would be to add a verse about cherry blossoms without losing the image of the forest of oaks. When he asked the Master to add a verse, this was how he did it.

Notes

BASHŌ

Introduction

Page 4

THE WAYS OF HOMOSEXUAL LOVE: Makoto Ueda, *Matsuo Bashō*, p. 22. In seventeenth century Japan *wakashudō* was "the way of homosexual love," *nyodō*, "the way of loving women." In town life romantic love was assumed to belong, not to marriage but to the theaters and wineshops, to the realm of prostitution, and no stigma attached to the choice between *wakashudō* and *nyodō*. *See* Paul Gordon Schalow's introduction to Ihara Saikaku, *The Great Mirror of Male Love*, Stanford University Press, 1990, a classic book of *wakashudō* stories from Bashō's time.

Page 7

TŌIN'S WIFE, JUTEI: Until very recently, the appearance of Jutei in Bashō's life had been a puzzle to biographers. Who was this woman he had taken into his care? In the nineteenth century, a book of eighteenth-century gossip turned up, written by someone who had been a student of someone who had been a student of a student of Bashō, which reported that Jutei had been Bashō's lover and that he was the father of her children. Legal records gave no indication that the children were his, but scholarship created and passed down the story of an early love between the young Bashō and the Buddhist nun. This conjecture turns up as fact in many accounts of Bashō's life, in both Japanese and English. Articles that refer to Bashō's love for Jutei have appeared in English language scholarly journals as recently as 1992. However, in 1991, a previously unknown letter by Bashō was discovered and published, which made it clear that Jutei was his nephew Tōin's wife.

Poems

The order of the poems is a little eccentric. The three on the first page are late. Pages 11 to 21 trace his early development chronologically. Then, because I wasn't sure he would approve of such an order, a random gathering of poems from different periods are presented on pages 22 to 36. On page 37, the chronological sequence resumes for Bashō's last years.

Page 11

EVEN IN KYOTO: The cuckoo *(Cuculus poliocephalus), hototogisu,* is in the haiku's vocabulary of seasonal symbols a summer bird. R. H. Blyth: "The breast of the male is blackish, with white blotches. The breast of the female is white, the inside of the mouth red. From early summer it sings day and night, ceases in autumn. It is said to vomit blood and die after it has sung eight thousand and eight times." *See Haiku* vol. 2, p. 161.

THIS ROAD: The word for road is *michi,* and Bashō wrote it in *kanji,* using the Chinese character, *tao,* rather than the Japanese phonetic signs for the two syllables. The poem may first of all be an evocation of the loneliness of this particular road, but Bashō's use of the ideogram suggests, as Robert Aitken has observed, that he also had in mind this other meaning. The Japanese also speak of *haiku no michi,* the way of the haiku poet, which suggests at least one other level of meaning.

THE WHITEBAIT: This is a late poem, and for Bashō unusually explicit. The law is dharma. But the first level of the poem has to do with perception. The eyes of the fish—the whitebait or sprat is silvery, about an inch and half long—look, in the net suddenly, as if their eyes had just opened, though fish, of course, don't close their eyes.

Page 12

FELLING A TREE: This early poem dates from 1677. According to Ueda, the lumberman's term for the cut end of the tree, *motokuchi*, may have had the more general meaning "origin" or "source" in Bashō's time.

Here are two other early poems of Bashō in the style of the school of Teimon:

> Foam on the wave's crest—
> blossoms of snow?
> the water's out-of-season flower?

The elaborate wordplay is typical. Literally, *Nami no hana to yuki mo ya mizu no kaeribana*. The Japanese idiom for the foam of a cresting wave is *nami no hana*, which means "blossom of the wave." In the last phrase of the poem, *mizu no kaeribana*, "water's out-of-season flower," *kaeribana* means "unseasonal flower," but *kaeri* means "returning," and so the incoming wave is also evoked. The punning makes many haiku, this one included, impossible to translate, and it was the style of writing, "a parlor game," Sam Hamill calls it, popular in Bashō's youth. And he was very good at it. *See* Ueda, *Bashō and His Interpreters*, p. 28.

> Smell of sake
> off the waves—
> the wine cup moon.

Tsuki, "moon," can also mean "wine cup." A literal translation: "Blue sea's wave / sake smell / today's moon (wine cup)." More wordplay, but even early there were these accuracies of perception, the rice-wine smell of the sea, the wave blue because the moon is full. *See* Ueda, p. 52.

And here is a poem Bashō wrote in the Danrin style, popular in Edo when he arrived there:

> Clouds passing over
> and—like a stray dog's peeing—
> scattered showers.

AUTUMN MOONLIGHT: Often cited as a turning point in Bashō's development, this was written in 1680. The headnote reads, "The later harvest moon," so it's an end-of-autumn poem. Ueda says that this moon is also called "the chestnut moon." For Japanese readers, this poem has a strongly Chinese flavor and reflects Bashō's immersion in Chinese poetry.

A SNOWY MORNING: Dried salmon, or salmon jerky, is ordinary food, neither rich nor poor.

Page 13

A CROW: This is one of Bashō's most famous poems. It also has a Chinese flavor for Japanese readers, probably because the Chinese painters, using black ink on white paper, were fond of drawing crows in winter. The verb here is everything: *tomari keri. Keri* signifies a completed action. The crow has just settled as the sky begins to grow dark.

ON THE WAY TO THE OUTHOUSE: Moonflowers bloom at night; the torch is probably oiled paper. Ueda comments that *kōka*, the word Basho uses, is a Zen term for "outhouse," so a monastery may be implied.

THE CRANE'S LEGS: Alludes to Chuang-tzu, the great Taoist teacher: "A wild duck has short legs but would be distressed if they were lengthened. A crane has long legs, but would be saddened if they were shortened." *See* Ueda, p. 73.

Page 14

WEATHERED BONES: This haiku introduces Bashō's first prose work, *Records of a Weathered Skeleton*, his account of his journey of 1684–1685. The prose preceding it evokes the old tradition of religious wanderers who set out with scant provisions and "entered a realm of perfect liberation, under the moon, late at night." *See* the discussion in Ueda, *Matsua Bashō*, pp. 125–26.

MISTY RAIN: The rain here is *kirishigure*, "mist-rain." A Japanese scholar, Tsutomo Ogata, on Japanese rain: "When my university was still free from campus disturbances, I used to read Bashō's *renku* with my colleagues from various departments, such as English literature, German literature, history, agriculture, etc. At one of those meetings Professor Hoshino Shin'ichi, a student of Rilke, commented: 'In Japanese there are many different words concerning rain which express the delicate shades of the seasons, such as *harusame* (spring rain), *samidare* (early summer rain), and *shigure* (the drizzling late autumn or early winter rain). The German word *regnen*, on the other hand, gives you the impression that it rains haphazardly in all seasons of the year. It would be almost impossible for those who are used to that sort of rain to appreciate haiku.'" This seems to me not entirely accurate, since both German and English are well-equipped to describe different kinds of rain: pour, drizzle, fall, sluice; spring rain, winter rain, hard rain, light rain, slanting rain, shower, and so on. What the remark points to is not a greater accuracy in Japanese, but a greater stylization. *Harusame* is automatically tender, *yūdachi*, "summer shower," is automatically sudden and refreshing, and so on. It seems likely that this aesthetic stylization bears the traces of an earlier animism, when *harusame* and *kirishigure* and *yūdachi* were thought of as nature spirits, particular beings. To some extent, in any case, the suggestive power of these short poems depends on this stylization.

Page 15

YOU'VE HEARD MONKEYS CRYING: See Ezra Pound's version of Li Po's "The River Merchant's Wife" in *Cathay*:

    At sixteen you departed,
    You went into far Ku-to-en, by the river of swirling eddies,

And you have been gone five months.
The monkeys make sorrowful noises overhead.

Or, variously, in Tu Fu, from the second poem in "Autumn Thoughts":

> True to the old song, my tears
> Drop as the gibbons cry.

Or, in Burton Watson's translation, from the "Seven Songs of T'ung-ku-hsien":

> I want to go in a little boat, but arrows fill my eyes.
> Far away in that southern land, banners of war abound.
> Ah-ah, song of the fourth, four times I've sung;
> Forest monkeys for my sake wail even at noon.

For a discussion of the child and Bashō's response, see Donald Keene, "Bashō's Journey of 1684," *Landscapes and Portraits.*

As for the hibiscus: *Mukuge* gets translated as "rose mallow" or "rose of Sharon." The mallows have maplelike leaves, flowers like hollyhocks. This species has white flowers and is tall, so Bashō's horse probably didn't even have to bend very far to crop it. Some mallows close in the shade. One western American species *(Hibiscus trionum)* is therefore called flower-of-an-hour.

It would melt: I have abbreviated Bashō's headnote.

Page 17

Spring: According to Ogata, Bashō has in mind the classical tradition of *utamakura*, poems about places with poetic, historical, or sacred associations. In this instance, he may have been thinking of these early *waka*, one from the *Manyōshù* and one by Gotaba-no-in from the *Shinkokinshū*.

> In the distance
> Kaguyama,
> The Heavenly Hill,
> Is misted over.
> Spring is here!

Spring must have come
Stealthily—

A mist trails over
The Heavenly Hill
Of Kaguyama.

A BUCKET OF AZALEAS: As in North America, azaleas, showy as they are, grow wild in the mountains. So this is a kind of genre scene, the sprigs of azalea in some kind of hanging bucket, the woman under them about her work.

Page 18

A BEE: The peony is a summer flower.

WHEN I LOOKED UNDER THE HEDGE: The weed, *nazuna*, is "shepherd's purse" in English, a member of the mustard family, named for the shape of its seedpods. It looks like a grass and produces tiny, white four-petaled flowers. A more literal translation: "When looking closely / *nazuna* flower / blooming in hedge!"

THE OLD POND: This is perhaps the best known of all haiku. A monument commemorates the place where Bashō is said to have composed it in the spring of 1686. The trick for translation is the last phrase: *mizu no oto*, literally, "sound of water." Translators have tried "water-sound," "plop," "splash," "glub," and the like. For one hundred separate English translations of this poem, see Hiroaki Sato, *One Hundred Frogs*. For my commentary, another frog jumping into the sea of commentary, *see* my essay "Looking for Rilke" in *Twentieth Century Pleasures*, The Ecco Press, 1984.

There is a story, repeated in many books about Bashō, that he wrote this poem spontaneously while being interrogated by a Zen monk, and achieved instant enlightenment, etc. In fact, he revised it several times, beginning with the frog leaping in the past tense, tentatively replacing "old pond" with "yellow roses blooming," and fiddling with several other small changes. *See* Earl Miner, *Japanese Linked Verse*, p. 96.

CLOUDS OF BLOSSOMS: They would be cherry blossoms. Plum for early spring, cherry, which symbolized its fullness, then pear, then peach for the mellow late spring. Ueno and Asakusa are temples in two different districts of Edo.

SICKLY: The chrysanthemum, white or yellow, was a fall flower. It was passionately and competitively cultivated and had associations with purity and with the royal family at Edo. Issa has a poem about a chrysanthemum that won in a chrysanthemum show and another about a chrysanthemum that came in second.

WINTER SUN: This is Ueda's translation, from *Bashō and His Interpreters*, p. 170. The alliteration and assonance in this poem are particularly admired: *fuyu no hi ya bajo ni koru kageboshi.*

A PETAL SHOWER: The phrase used to describe the falling petals is onomatopoeic: *horohoro.* Some connection between that sound and the sound of the river.

EXCITING AT FIRST: People liked to watch the cormorant fishermen on moonless summer nights using their birds to fish. The birds were leashed, with rings fastened to their throats to keep them from swallowing the catch.

BLOWING STONES: Bashō's successive revisions of this poem survive. The first version read: "Autumn wind! / blowing down the stones / on Mount Asama." The second: "The blasting downwind— / on Asama a storm / of stones." This is tinkered with. The third reads: "Stones blown down— / this is the autumn storm / of Asama!" *See* Keene, "Bashō's Journey to Sarashina," *Landscapes and Portraits.*

SEEING PEOPLE OFF: This translation is by R. H. Blyth, *Haiku,* vol. 3, p. 122. Aitken observes that a literal translation might read: "Seeing people off, being seen off, and the upshot is autumn in Kiso."

Page 24

AS THE SOUND FADES: Literally, the scent of the flowers strikes, or rings.

HOW ADMIRABLE!: As Robert Aitken observes, the central phrase, *satorenu no hito,* can be translated as "one's not being enlightened, or experiencing *satori.*" So: How noble / the person not enlightened / by lightning. Bashō's headnote suggests it was directed against Zen faddists. Roland Barthes, in *The Empire of Signs,* suggests that it is a send-up of the whole system of cultural signification on which haiku, and cultures in general, are based. That is, what's enlightened is to see "nothing that is not there and the nothing that is."

Page 25

THE SQUID SELLER'S CALL: Squid seller = summer; cuckoo = summer.

BY THE OLD TEMPLE: Peach blossoms, hence the mellow late spring.

Page 27

A CICADA SHELL: This translation is by Blyth, *Haiku,* vol. 3, p. 235.

Page 29

HAILSTONES: Hard things hitting hard things in a hard place. Mountain passes were mysterious places in old Japanese culture, inhabited by boundary gods and placatory shrines, sometimes with the carved figure of a man and a woman coupling.

Page 31

A CALM MOON: This is a very late poem, written at a haiku party ten days or so before Bashō's death. The subject for the night was love. Love was a required theme of the thirty-six-verse *kasen* sequences, and one imagines the purpose of the party was to practice these verses. They often appeared at about the twenty-fourth or twenty-fifth position in the sequence. Another hokku by Bashō on this subject is spoken by a woman.

> Let my cruel lover
> crawl to me
> through the quince hedge.

Quince bushes have sharp spikes.

The word *chigo*, which Ueda translates as "handsome youth" and "boy-lover," refers to the younger partner in a pair of male lovers. As in ancient Athens, the typical relationship in Bashō's time was between an older and a younger man. Foxes, in Japanese folklore, were mischievous and had supernatural powers. The speaker in the poem is escorting the frightened boy home.

NOT THIS HUMAN SADNESS: Literally, "I feel sorrow *(uki)* / make me feel loneliness *(sabishi)* or solitariness / cuckoo!" The bird he addresses is the mountain cuckoo, the *kankadori*, which has a beautiful song and is rarely seen.

SAD BEAUTY: The word I've translated with this phrase, perhaps awkwardly, is *aware*, "pathos, feeling."

Page 32

HAVING PLANTED A BANANA TREE: The tree is the *bashō*, from which the poet took his pen name. *See* Donald Shively's wonderful essay on Bashō and the *bashō*, "Bashō, the Man and the Plant."

Page 35

A FISHY SMELL: Intense summer heat is implied.

Page 36

LIFE IN THIS WORLD: The headnote is Ueda's translation. This is an evocation of Bashō's pantheon, the Sung poet Su Tung-p'o (1037–1101) and Tu Fu (712–770), greatest of Chinese lyric poets; Saigyō (1118–1190), medieval Japanese monk and *waka* poet; and Sōgi (1421–1502), also a Zen poet. They are all types of the poet as pilgrim and ascetic.

Page 37

MORE THAN EVER I WANT TO SEE: Blyth: "There was a story that En no Otsuno, a necromancer, born in 634, when intending to make a bridge between Katsuragi and Yoshino, asked a god, Hitokoto-nushi, to help him. The god's face was so hideous that he appeared only at night." *History of Haiku,* vol. 1, p. 116.

HEAT WAVES SHIMMERING: The grass is still dead, the earth just heating up. The barest hint of spring.

Page 38

SPRING GOING: This poem opens *Narrow Road to the Far North;* it was composed on May 16, 1689, and echoes some lines of Tu Fu.

> Grieving for the times, I weep at the sight of flowers.
> Resentful of parting, I think of the cries of birds.

It's another poem of departure. They left their friends at Senju, a fishing village. Bashō and his companion Sora are perhaps the birds. The poem begins with the phrase *yuku haru,* "spring ending." The last poem in *Narrow Road* (see p. 42) ends with the phrase *yuku aki,* "fall ending." Here is Cid Corman's evocative translation of the headnote:

Last of March, slightly hazy dawn, 'a waning moon, a falling light' (quoted from *Genji*), summit of Fuji vague, crowns of blossoming cherry of Ueno and Yanaka, when would they—and would they—be seen again? Friends, gathering since nightfall, came along by boat to see us off, sense of three thousand *li* ahead swelling the heart, world so much a dream, tears at point of departure.

THE BEGINNING OF ART: The word I've translated as "art" is *fūryū*, which implies courtliness, elegance, good taste. The songs Bashō was hearing were ancient and traditional, and probably did reach back to the beginnings of poetry as magical incantation. The poem was written at Sukagawa, which marked the entrance to Japan's northern and wilder provinces. It begins the journey proper. *See* Sam Hamill's discussion of this poem in *Bashō's Ghost*, pp. 22–23.

Page 39

CHESTNUT BY THE EAVES: This *haibun* gets the carefulness of Bashō's method in *Narrow Road*. It looks as casual as the work of Frank O'Hara, but he is working emblematically, like an English Renaissance poet. First the priest living under a chestnut at the edge of town. Then the memory of a poem from Saigyō's reclusion.

> Deep in the mountains,
> sipping clear water
> from a mountain stream,
> gathering horse chestnuts
> fallen here and there.

And from the poet-monk, living on brook water and fallen chestnuts, to Gyōgi Bosatsu (670–749), an early Japanese Buddhist wanderer and holy man, later a high priest. In the folk tradition he had magical healing powers—like Saigyō, who is supposed to have once cured a child by reciting a poem—and special powers as a seer. From his attachment to the wood of the chestnut Bashō leaps to a derivation of the name of the tree that associates it with the Western Paradise (a condition of being, not a geographical place) of Pure Land Buddhism. And then a glimpse at the chestnut blossoms unnoticed above the eaves of a busy border town. For a discussion of this poem, *see* William La Fleur, *The Karma of the Word* pp. 149–64.

FLEAS, LICE: Ueda observes that the verb *shitosuru* refers to children's urination. I first rendered this "pissing"; Blyth and Ueda use "piddling," which isn't American English to my ear.

Page 40

STILLNESS: The headnote is from Cid Corman's translation of *Narrow Road*.

Page 41

WANTING TO SAIL: The *haibun* on this page is also from *Narrow Road*. It finds Bashō in a rural village in the mountains, where there is a passion for linked verse and the writing is so old-fashioned, and therefore moving, that it puts him in mind of the barbarian reed pipes heard on the borders of the empire by Tang poets like Tu Fu. From the tradition of poetry as a river to the river itself, swift, used for backcountry transport, to the temple, tranquilly detached from its force, standing near the falls. And then the verse, about the spring waters, which reverberates in lots of different ways.

Page 42

A WILD SEA: Commentators speak of the grandeur of this poem, which I'm afraid my translation doesn't get. Sado Island was an island for political exiles, of grim or melancholy association. Thus, the rough seas, the penal island (where gold was mined), and a strewing of stars in the heavens.

STAYING AT AN INN: Bashō and Sora are presumably "the moon." I have always thought this poem was condescending, but the commentators (*see* Ueda, p. 261) emphasize the sense of parallel

---

lives, temporary shelter, different worlds coming and going. A friendly, though distant, relation, like a bright moon in the night sky and the gleam of clover in the field.

The courtesans, or prostitutes, are *yūjo*. And it is hard to know how to translate the word. For an account of the distinctions between *maiko* (apprentice geishas), *geisha,* and *yūjo,* see Liza Dalby, *Geisha,* Berkeley: University of California Press, 1983. Geishas were trained in the arts and in social graces, yūjos in *toko no higi,* the techniques of sexual pleasure.

Page 43

ALONG THE SHORE: Literally, "interval between waves / small shells mixed in / the debris of bush clover." A fall poem, written on the beach at Iro: empty shells and fallen petals, or shell bits that look like dried petals at the boundary between land and sea. Blyth translates the first line, "in the surf," suggesting a wave roiling the two kinds of flotsam indistinguishably.

FALL GOING: This is the last poem in *Narrow Road* and echoes the poem that opens the book. It is more than usually impossible to translate, and I kept it simple. The poem reads: *hamaguri no futami ni wakare yuku aki zo. Hamaguri* is "clam." *Futami* is a bay famous for its clams and its views. Its name means "two views" or "two looks." But *futa* also means "lid," and thus *hamaguri no futa* is "clam's lid"; and *mi* can be both "see," hence a pun on "eyelid," and "meat or flesh," hence the meat of the clam. *Wakare* is "parting" or "farewell." Cid Corman's translation: "clam / shell and innards parting / departing fall." Earl Miner: "Parting for Futami Bay / Is like tearing the body from the clamshell / Autumn goes to its end." Yuasa: "As firmly cemented clamshells / Fall apart in autumn / So I must take to the road again, / Farewell, my friends." Blyth: "Autumn / Parting we go, clams opening, / to Futami." Stryk: "Futami friends, farewell— / clam torn from shell, / I follow autumn." I once tried a freer version: "Fall is ending / and we part—like eyelids, / like clams opening."

Page 44

FROM ALL THESE TREES: This translation is Sam Hamill's, from *Bashō's Ghost*, p. 21.

Page 45

A GROUP OF THEM: Robert Aitken reads this as a humorous poem about an unprepossessing lot of haiku poets, Bashō among them, at a moon-viewing party. I have taken it as a more neutral assessment of a group of strangers.

COLD NIGHT: THE WILD DUCK: Bashō had caught a bad cold at Lake Biwa on one of his expeditions. He may implicitly be speaking about his own situation, as he often does.

Page 47

DON'T IMITATE ME: More literally, "don't resemble me / split in two / muskmelon." According to Ueda, "a melon split in half" is an idiomatic expression for two persons who are almost identical. The melon gives the poem its seasonal reference, that is, ripeness is all, but one's own ripeness.

Page 48

SAD NODES: For the setting of this poem in *haibun* see "The Hut of the Phantom Dwelling." *Fushi* is the node of the bamboo stalk from which the new leaves spring. According to Ueda, the word also came to mean any juncture, or a mathematical point.

PINE MUSHROOM: *matsudake*, a shelf fungus (edible) that grows on pine trees.

Page 49

BUSH WARBLER: The name of the bird is *uguisu*; it's associated with spring and in painting with plum blossoms. About the size of a sparrow, though slimmer, olive green and dusty white, sprightly, with a melodious song. There is a wonderful story about the *uguisu* and about Japanese attention to natural phenomena in Burton Watson's *The Rainbow World* (pp. 81–82):

The same evening, I asked a Japanese friend if he knew the identity of the bird I had heard making such a wild cry, reproducing the cry for him as I had rehearsed it in the mountains. My friend showed immediate signs of comprehension. "*Uguisu no tani-watari*," he said.

"So it was an *uguisu*," I exclaimed.

He nodded.

"And what does *tani-watari* mean?"

It's the cry the *uguisu* makes when he is crossing over from one valley to another."

I stared incredulously. A special word for one particular type of cry made by one particular species of bird? One has heard that some languages have highly specialized terminology in certain areas of reference, but this seemed too much to believe. I rushed to another room to consult my Japanese-English dictionary. There it was in Kenkyusha in unmistakable print: "*tani-watari*—the song of a bush warbler flying from valley to valley."

Page 50

CATS MAKING LOVE: The poem is about the quiet after the yowling.

Page 51

THE MORNING GLORY ALSO: The headnote reads, "Around the time I closed the gate of my house in Fukagawa." The poem is as cryptic as it appears to be.

STILL ALIVE: The shore in winter; sea slugs are usually a humorous subject in Japanese verse.

Page 52

LIGHTNING FLASH: This is a dance-of-the-dead poem; in a flash the faces have become ghostly weeds.

LIGHTNING: Night herons were associated with the uncanny.

THIS AUTUMN: Written ten days or so before his death. The middle phrase is *nande toshiyoru,* also possibly, "why am I so old?" or "why do we grow old?" Robert Aitken translates it in *A Zen Wave,* "Somehow I have grown old." The last phrase is *kumo ni tori,* literally, "to the clouds, a bird." Commentators have found it inexpressibly poignant. I can't find, and haven't seen, an adequate rendering.

Page 54

SICK ON A JOURNEY: Bashō's last poem, dictated to a disciple on November 24, 1694. He died on the twenty-sixth.

Prose

Two examples of Bashō's prose are included here, both late. "The Hut of the Phantom Dwelling" was written after his return from the long journey to the north, in the summer of 1690, in a small mountain cottage prepared for him by his students in Zeze, a town on the shore of Lake Biwa. *The Saga Diary* dates from the spring of the following year, when he stayed for two weeks at a villa owned by his disciple and friend Kyorai at Saga on the northwest outskirts of Kyoto. It is the last of his major prose works. For a discussion of both works and of the style of Bashō's *haibun,* see Ueda, *Matsuo Bashō.*

"The Hut of the Phantom Dwelling"

Page 55

HACHIMAN: "In Bashō's time the Buddhist and Shinto religions had become so interfused that it was not uncommon for a Buddhist statue to be worshiped in a shrine dedicated to a Shinto deity." Burton Watson, from *Eight Islands.* There is another

---

English translation of this piece, based on a somewhat different text, by Donald Keene, in *Anthology of Japanese Literature*.

The Saga Diary

Page 60

LADY KOGO: A lady of the court of the Emperor Takakura (1168–1180); the emperor took an interest in her, and his wife's father, Kiyomori, had her banished from the court. The story appears in *Tales of Heike*, and the minister Nakakuni's search for the banished lady was dramatized in a No play.

Page 66

HUANG TING-CHIEN: A Sung dynasty poet.

FIVE-BU CANDLESTICK: A *renga* written in the time it took for a candle to burn down five *bu*, or half an inch.

Page 67

The entry for the twenty-sixth is a glimpse of the practice of linked verse. From persimmon seeds to blossoms, from scattered blossoms to the snail's waving horns, and so on.

Page 68

TOKOKU: Bashō's student had died the year before at the age of thirty.

Page 69

BRIDEGROOM'S CAKE: A rice cake given by the bridegroom to the bride's parents during the time of the fifth moon.

BUSON

Introduction

Page 74

SHIKI: Masaoka Shiki (1867–1902) wrote a series of essays about Buson in the 1890s as well as a famous attack on the veneration of Bashō: "Bashō's haiku have acquired a power virtually identical to that of a religion. His many believers do not necessarily follow him because of his character or conduct, nor do they respond to him because they have read his poems." For an account, *see* Janine Beichman, *Masaoka Shiki*, Twayne, NY: 1982. One side of Shiki's Buson is not reflected very well in my selections. Attacking Bashō for his subjectivity—"Bashō's haiku speak only of what was around him"—he praised Buson for including in his subject matter "scenes which arise from imagination and are outside observation, as well as human affairs he himself had not experienced." As instances, Shiki cited Buson's use of the stuff of folklore in haiku such as these translated by Beichman.

> An inn for
> kappa to make love in—
> the summer moon.

> Harvest moon—
> a rabbit crossing
> Suwa Lake.

Kappa are legendary river beasts; the moon on the water is their inn. The rabbit in the second poem is the one in folklore that beats rice cakes on the moon. Buson also wrote poems that were, in effect, historical and dramatic tableaux, the most famous of which are probably these.

> Asking for a night's lodging
> swords are thrown down—
> a heavy snowstorm!

> In the bedroom, stepping
> on my dead wife's comb:
> the sudden cold.

The first poem imagines a troop of samurai of the elder days storming into an inn. Shiki also praised Buson for his painterly detachment, pictorial precision, and delicacy.

KEMA: The letter written on the twenty-third day of the second month, 1777, appears in Yuki Sawa and Edith Shiffert, *Haiku Master Buson*, p. 170.

THERE IS A STORY: Writing twenty-five years after Buson's death, an Osaka writer said, "Buson squandered the fortune of his fore-fathers, lived a carefree and uninhibited life, and wandered far from the teachings of the gods, the Buddha, and holy men. He was a vagabond who sold his fame and flattered the common people." Sawa and Shiffert, *Haiku Master Buson*, p. 31; Eri Fujita Yasuhara, *"Buson and Haishi,"* p. 19.

Page 75

WENJEN: I am condensing the brilliant discussion of these issues in Mark Morris's "Buson and Shiki, Part One." Morris makes the interesting observation that the *wenjen* and *bunjin* painters established the legitimacy of painting as an art by moving away from representation. He quotes James Cahill: "The quality of a painting, said the literati artists, reflects the personal qualities of the artist; its expressive content derives from his mind, and has no necessary relationship to anything the artist or viewer thinks or feels about the object represented." And he tells the story of a Chinese painter Ni Tsan, to whom a critic said that his bamboo didn't look like bamboo at all. Ni Tsan replied, "Ah, but a total lack of resemblance is hard to achieve, not everyone can manage it." This is interesting in relation to Buson's famous objectivity. It's not the same thing as representational accuracy.

Page 76

READ CHINESE POETRY: Buson had in mind the *Mustard Seed Manual*, a Chinese manual important to Japanese painters of the period: "In painting there is only one way to rid yourself of the vulgar: read much, and the force of the volumes read will increase within you while the force of commercial vulgarity will decline."

Page 77

THOSE WHO DOMINATE THE HAIKAI WORLD: quoted by Yasuhara, "Buson and Haishi" p. 33.

Page 78

KITŌ: "A Record of Buson's Last Days," in Sawa and Shiffert, *Haiku Master Buson*, pp. 45–50.

EARLY SPRING: *See* my version on page 125. Another translation is:

> From this night on
> every day will dawn
> in white plum blossoms.

This has been read as a Jōdo Buddhist sentiment. Thus, the white blossoms are the Paradise of the West. But it has also, as in Bashō's death poem, been read as a statement about his art: I have become my poems.

Poems

Page 81

THE TWO PLUM TREES: This is R. H. Blyth's translation. Literally, the two branches of plum. It's also an instance of the way Buson mixes, or fuses, Chinese and Japanese elements in his poems. This one uses a Chinese expression, *chisoku*, "slow-fast," with a classical Japanese seasonal phrase, *ume*, "plum." And the verb "to love" is written with the Chinese character rather than with the Japanese phonetic signs. It's very characteristic Buson. Instead of the expected phrase, *hana no ume,* one gets the surprising and unusual specification *Futa moto no ume,* "two branches of plum," then the Chinese word *chisoku,* then the Japanese verb *aisu* written with the Chinese ideogram, and then the traditional concluding phrase *kana,* which is usually translated with an exclamation point in English.

Futa moto no ume ni /	two branches of plum in /
chisoku wo /	slow-fast (accusative) /
aisu kana	I love!

All haiku poets used *kanji,* the Chinese ideograms, to some extent, but Buson apparently gives the feeling of writing a kind of Sino-Japanese, perhaps in the way the early Wallace Stevens wrote a French symbolist English or the way Walter Savage Landor wrote his exquisite epigrams in English Latin. Aesthetically, as with Stevens and Landor, this manner conveys a sense at once of playfulness and of taking the high road of serious art against folksy, popular, bourgeois writing. One can try to render Buson's unusual precision, but this other effect, of course, can't be conveyed.

Page 82

WHITE BLOSSOMS OF THE PEAR: As Blyth remarks, white pear blossoms, white face in the moonlight, white paper, white moon. She's outside, so it's a love letter.

Page 84

PLUMS IN BLOSSOM: I've used *geisha* here as a shorthand. Literally, *Muro no yūjo,* "the courtesans of Muro." The *yūjo* were prostitutes regulated by the government; they lived in an entertainment quarter of the city and were not permitted to leave it. The women in the poem can't go out and look at the blossoms, so they buy sashes with blossoms on them for their rooms. Geishas, unlike *yūjo,* were trained in music and the social refinements and were, at least in law, not sexually available.

THE OLD CORMORANT KEEPER: In the summer people liked watching the cormorant fishermen on the embankments handling their birds.

APPRENTICE'S DAY OFF: Once a year in feudal Japan apprentices got a day off to go home, during the season for kite flying. The boy in the poem is going home. The kite, implied but not seen, tugging in the wind, is the buried metaphor.

Page 85

LIGHTING ONE CANDLE: It's spring; the night is so mild, the people (or person) in the poem don't go to bed when the candle gutters, which good sense and economy would dictate. Another candle is lit on the first one, and the flaring of the new wick is the metaphor for spring.

TEARS: "Hazy moon" is an autumn *kigo*. Another instance of Buson's youthful chinoiserie. He has in mind an old Chinese poem:

Returning Wild Geese

Why do they so blindly depart from Shosho?
The water is blue, the sand is white, the moss
    on both banks green;
Should the lute of twenty-five strings be played,
    on a moonlit night,
With the overwhelming emotion, will they not
    return?

This is Blyth's translation. A romantic story is attached to the Chinese poem. *See* Blyth's discussion in *Haiku*, vol. 1, p. 51. He is a little indignant: "Buson's verse is literature...but it is not haiku."

Page 86

THE SPRING SEA RISING: This poem is admired for its sound: *Haru no umi hinemosu notari notari kana.*

EARLY SUMMER RAIN: This poem also has a Chinese accent. Mark Morris says, nicely, that it "teases with the possibility of a very Japanese rain, the rain of *samidare,* falling on a scene set inside a Chinese landscape" (p. 415). The houses are seen at a distance, across the river in the rain. Their exposure to rising water seems to be hinted at. The last phrase has been translated, "two lone houses."

SICK MAN PASSING: Barley was harvested in the summertime.

SOUND OF A SAW: The sound so late at night, hence poor people.

A FIELD OF MUSTARD: This is a field of *na,* rapeseed, and "rape blossoms" seems impossible in English. The flowers are bright yellow, so I transposed the species, same genus, from rape to mustard, since, on the Pacific coast, it is the acid-yellow mustard that appears when the whales migrate.

THE SOUND OF A BELL: A mountain temple in the original.

THE SHORT NIGHT: *Mijakayo* is the seasonal phrase for the short summer night. Buson always writes on this subject from the point of view of early morning, as if the world were being born. These poems remind me a bit of the European *alba,* the lovers' dawn song, and there is a similar tradition in the classical *waka.* Though the haiku tradition is supposed to avoid erotic themes,

---

I've wondered if these weren't about making love through the short summer night and then walking home as the light resolves itself into a world. "patrolmen / washing in the river" and "a broom thrown away / on the beach" are Blyth's translations; several of the others are variants of his.

Page 99

THE SHORT NIGHT: The dawn light is just faintly illuminating the screen by the bed.

EVENING WIND: Spring; the Japanese grey heron looks a lot like the North American great blue.

Page 103

A DAY SLOW IN GOING: This poem is admired for its sound: *Osoki hi ya kodama kikoyuru kyo no sumi.*

Page 104

BUYING LEEKS: Leeks are a winter vegetable.

Page 107

A DOG BARKING: The village is so far in the sticks that dogs bark at the unusual event of a peddler, so far that the roads are impassable until the peach trees bloom. This is waking-up-in-spring-very-slowly, or taking-a-long-time-for-the-meaning-of-a-poem-to-dawn-on-you.

THE OWNER OF THE FIELD: This translation is by Jorie Graham.

Page 108

THE LIGHTS ARE GOING OUT: The Doll Festival was an annual spring event, and doll markets sprung up. Here they're closing down at the end of the day.

Bats flitting here and there: It's a summer night. This has something in common with William Carlos Williams' "The Young Housewife."

Remembering him: Written on the anniversary of the death of Watanabe Unribo (1693?–1761). The headnote, from a letter, is translated by Leon Zolbrod in "The Busy Year," p. 70.

The willow leaves fallen: Among Buson's poems, this was one of his own personal favorites and he made several drawings of the rocks. The poem has elaborate echoes. It was originally written to start a renga; later Buson added a headnote: "About the beginning of the tenth month I was travelling through Shimotsuke; there beneath the shade of the tree called Pilgrim's Willow, I expressed the scene before my eyes." This willow is the subject of a *waka* by Saigyō:

> Under a willow
> in the North Country
> where a fresh spring flowed—
> I meant to stay
> only a little while.

As Saigyō's tree, it figures in a No play, *Yugyo yanagi,* and in *Narrow Road to the Far North* Bashō records his visit there: "The willow about which Saigyō wrote the famous *waka* still stood by the rice field in Ashino village:

> They planted a whole field
> before I left it—
> the willow."

Later when Buson made a fan on which he inscribed the poem, he drew on it a scattering of rocks and alluded to a prose poem, "Second Journey to the Red Cliff," by Su Tung-p'o (1037–1101), the Sung poet-painter, which reads in part:

So we took the wine and fish and went on another
excursion under the Red Cliff. The river flowed
noisily, the banks rose sheer for a thousand feet;
the moon was small between the high mountains, and
stones stood out from the sunken water; even after
so few months river and mountains were no longer
recognizable.

See Mark Morris, "Buson and Shiki: Part Two," pp. 299–303,
and Calvin French, *The Poet Painters*, pp. 74–75.

THE PETALS FALL: Some lines from Li Po:

Peach blossoms on the flowing water,
  At once they're swept away.

See Morris, "Buson and Shiki, Part Two," pp. 310–11.

Page 115

THE MOUNTAIN CUCKOO: The *kankodori,* or Himalayan cuckoo
(Cuculus sataratus), is a summer visitor to the mountains of Ja-
pan. It lives in deep forests, has a call like that of a pigeon but
louder, and is often heard but rarely seen. The tradition about it
was that no one knew anything about it.

Page 117

CALLIGRAPHY OF GEESE: The moon is like the owner's red stamp in
the corner of a scroll painting.

IT CRIED THREE TIMES: Fall, the rutting season.

Page 124

THE OLD CALENDAR: This is Blyth's translation. The "old calen-
dar" was a farmer's almanac full of Shinto folk legends, Taoist
lucky numbers, moral and practical advice, etc.

Page 125

WINTER WARBLER: Kitō writes in "A Record of Buson's Last
Days": "On the night of the twenty-fourth, his sick body was

---

very calm, and his speaking voice became natural again. Quietly he called Gekkei near him and said, 'I made some poems during my sickness. Write them down quickly.' Brush and inkstone were prepared." Sawa and Shiffert, p. 48. This poem and the next were two of the three he dictated. Wang Wei was the Tang poet-painter, one of Buson's artistic models.

IN THE WHITE PLUM BLOSSOMS: This poem is difficult to translate. Blyth: "Every night from now / will dawn / from the white plum tree." Sawa and Shiffert: "With white plum blossoms / these nights to the faint light of dawn / are turning." Morris: "Now each and every night will end / Dawning in white plum blossoms." Buson: *Shiraume ni akuru yo bakari to nari ni keri.*

Long Poems

Japanese poets worked in the *renga, waka,* and haiku forms; they also composed poems in Chinese well into the nineteenth century. In the history of Japanese literature, there is very little precedent for these three poems by Buson, and not much like them afterwards, until Japanese poets began to experiment with European verse forms early in the twentieth century. One is an elegy in free verse, one is an elegiac and erotic lyric written in a combination of Chinese and Japanese, and one, the longest, fuses haiku, Chinese quatrains, and stanzas that combine elements of both into a lyrical narrative poem that is certainly a sport and some think a masterpiece of Japanese poetry.

The Japanese name for these free-form poems is *haishi.* My annotations of them depend on Eri Fujita Yasuhara's fascinating study "Buson and Haishi: A Study of Free-Form Haikai Poetry in Eighteenth Century Japan," a doctoral dissertation she completed at UCLA in 1982.

"Mourning for Hokuju Rosen"

Hokuju was the pen name of Hayami Shinga, a *haikai* poet and wealthy sake brewer from Yuki whom Buson knew in the poetry circles of Edo. He died in 1754 at the age of seventy-four, when Buson was twenty-nine. The poem was probably written in that year and was found among Buson's papers and published twelve years after his death. It's a free-verse poem written in Japanese. A few other Edo poets of the period experimented with *haishi,* but none of them seems a likely model for this poem, and it's not clear that Buson was aware of the other poems, though he could have been.

The poem is fairly straightforward, but Japanese critics have been puzzled by two things: the time sequence and the description of the smoke in line 9, *hege no keburi.* No one is sure what *hege* means, and solutions include the smoke from a stove, smoke from bamboo shavings, smoke from the funeral ceremony, etc. Recently a Japanese scholar, Tonotsugo Muramatsu, proposed the novel thesis that the smoke was smoke from a flint-lock rifle and that the rifle had killed the pheasant in the poem and that the surviving pheasant speaks lines 8 through 13. Which makes the poem sound remarkably similar to Walt Whitman's "Out of the Cradle Endlessly Rocking" with its grieving mockingbird. Yasuhara has made a version of the poem based on that theory:

> You went away this morning—tonight my heart is torn in a
> thousand pieces
> Why are you so far?
> Thinking of you I wandered to the hill
> Why is the hill so sad?
> Dandelions are blooming yellow—the shepherd's purse
> white
> But no one to see them.
> Is that a pheasant? I hear its mournful cry.
> "I too had a friend who lived across the river.
> Mysterious smoke suddenly burst forth—a strong wind rose
> and
> Among the reeds and grasses
> No one could find refuge.
> I too had a friend who lived across the river, but today

He does not cry even a single note."
You went away this morning—tonight my heart is torn in a
    thousand pieces
Why are you so far?
This dusk in my hut, lighting no candle before the Amida
Offering no flowers, I stand with a heavy heart
Yet how precious is this moment.

"Song of the Yodo River"

Another experiment. The first two stanzas, spoken by a woman, are written in five-word Chinese quatrains, the last, spoken by a man, in Japanese, "like a quatrain written out in Japanese syntax," says Yasuhara. This poem and the following one, both set in the countryside of Buson's home district, were published by Buson in 1777, when he was sixty-two years old. An earlier version of the poem contains a headnote that reads: "On behalf of a courtesan seeing off a man returning to Naniwa after he was entertained at the Tower of a Hundred Blossoms in Fushimi." Fushimi is on the Uji River, which flows into the Yodo and from there into Osaka Bay. Naniwa is the old name for Osaka.

The imagery of the poem and the theme are fairly conventional, and Buson had used the image of plum petals being swept downriver in a haiku—not just transience, but fast transience. The interest of the poem is in the contrast of styles and speakers. The courtesan, with her rigidly controlled life, longs for love and sees her lover as passing beauty. More poignantly, she longs to have a life. She says, literally, in the last line, "and become a person *(hito)* of Naniwa forever." Yasuhara translates the line, "citizen of Naniwa." The courtesan wants a real life outside the walls. The male speaker sees *her* as the plum blossoms, the suddenly passing beauty he can't have. He is "a person of Naniwa," for which his metaphor is the rooted willow with its shadow sunk in the fast-moving water.

MOORING ROPE: *Kinran,* literally, "brocade line." Yasuhara comments that it could be an allusion to the cord that binds her robe and that this, together with the reference to lightning, suggests a plea to the lover to delay their too ravenous lovemaking.

"Spring Wind on the Riverbank at Kema"

Also published in 1777, this is the most unexpected and unparalleled of Buson's three experiments in *haishi.* It has a prose preface and is written in a mixture of Japanese haiku, Chinese quatrains, and stanzas that contain elements of both. Specifically, it comprises five haiku, four Chinese quatrains, one tanka, and eight verses in free forms. The fact that it contains eighteen stanzas is probably not incidental. The linked-verse form that Buson worked in, the *kasen,* contained thirty-six stanzas. Buson made two comments about the poem. In a letter to a friend, he said that he arranged the poem "like the moving backdrop of a play" and that it "welled up from an old man's uncontrollable longing for the past."

Its theme is the plangent one to Japanese of return to the home village. The speaker is a country girl from Buson's town of Kema who has gone to Naniwa (Osaka) to work in service for a wealthy family. Yasuhara's commentary notices a second theme, the kittenish sexiness and self-consciousness of the young woman with her new big-city sophistication in the opening sections giving way as the poem progresses to a pure yearning for the mother's body.

Japanese critics, as a kind of subtheme of this erotic theme, have read the poem as Buson's psychological study of himself. Attracted to the young woman, he begins to enter her world, and as he does, his own desire for his childhood village and his mother overrides the flirtatious occasion of the poem and leaves him in the poetry of "uncontrollable longing." Yasuhara is inclined, in fact, to read the two poems as a kind of narrative: first, in "Song of the Yodo River," the double bind of an erotic affair, and then, in "Spring Wind on the Riverbank at Kema" a study of its purest source. In the volume in which the two poems appear, edited by Buson, they follow one another and are followed by a haiku that ends the volume:

> Spring going—
> ah! the warbler,
> its voice of old.

The warbler is the *uguisu*, the traditional harbinger of spring. So this is a kind of envoi to desire and to promise. The biographical critics notice that Buson's only daughter married the same year the poems were composed and that a few years later he was writing to a friend to say, "Following your advice, today I will give up my longing for Koito [a geisha, presumably]. Because of my useless romantic feeling, I've lost my dignity in my old age."

Whatever one thinks of all this, the suggestion about the two themes of the poem helps one to see how wonderfully the pace is managed and how it begins to quicken at about the tenth section toward its conclusion.

Page 131

NEW YEAR'S HOLIDAY: Literally, *yabuiri*, a traditional three-day leave given to serving girls, usually on the sixteenth day of the New Year, two days for travel, one day to spend with their families. Nagara was an older, country person's name for the river.

Page 132

LEAVING THE BANK: Yasuhara comments on the vaguely erotic and self-conscious tone of stanzas three and four. The Chinese quatrains slow the poem down as she dallies.

A SOLITARY TEAHOUSE: The haiku with its traditional imagery as she approaches the world of her village past.

THE OLD WOMAN: New Year's was the time for gifts of new clothes. The country woman is admiring her city style, and she reports on it happily.

Two men: There are different theories about "the language of the southern riverside." According to one, it is country speech; according to another, it is the slang of the entertainment quarter, in which case she is reporting that two city dudes with money in their pockets have noticed how pretty she is. In either case, they've noticed.

Page 133

Old farmhouses: Another haiku, and the last until the one that ends the poem. In one interpretation, this subsumes the erotic theme, "no mate," and intensifies the nostalgic one, "old farmhouses." And the next section introduces the theme of the mother.

Page 134

Dandelions blooming: The counting apparently echoes some childhood game. She remembers leaving home.

Long, long ago: The classical tanka form, which was felt to be more dignified than the haiku.

Page 136

Do you remember: Taiga was a contemporary of Buson and, after him, the most distinguished *haikai* poet of the era.

New Flower Picking

Buson did not work much in prose and scholars agree that he is at his best in his letters. *New Flower Picking* is his one extended prose work. He wrote it in 1777. Intending it originally as an album of hokku, he set himself the task of writing ten each day. After a while he left off and turned to prose sketches and small essays, including these anecdotal tales about mysterious badgers and foxes. Tales of the supernatural were popular in the mid-eighteenth century; Akinari Ueda, the author of the greatest of

---

them, *Ugetsu Monogatari*, was a friend of Buson. The prose is not his finest work, but it gives a glimpse of another side of his character and of his time.

Page 139

AUTUMN AGAIN (HANGING DOWN): An instance of the kind of punning haiku can sustain.

ISSA

Introduction

Page 146

BUSON'S WORK: Blyth, in *History of Haiku* vol. 1 (p. 354), gives three examples of Issa's early poems written in the manner of Buson.

> Only the pagoda
> of Toji Temple visible
> among the summer groves.

> A fire of dead twigs;
> the shadow on the window
> of a woman spinning.

> Her face reflected
> in the oil of the lamp—
> burning mosquitoes

Page 147

PURE LAND BUDDHIST: *Jōdo-shū*, Pure Land Buddhism, was founded in the twelfth century by a monk named Honen. One of his students, Shinran, left monastic life and founded the sect to which Issa's family belonged, *Jōdo-shin-shū*, or *Shin-shū*. Shin-shū Buddhism was a purely lay community with no monastic practice. The essence of the teaching was the veneration of Amida through the recitation of the formula *Namu Amida butsu*, "Veneration to Buddha Amitabha." Said with complete faith and devotion, the phrase itself could bring about rebirth in the Pure Land of Amida. Shin-shū Buddhists were encouraged to adapt themselves to the world and to rely on faith, not works. Now the most important school of Buddhism in Japan— "mainline, middle-class, Mahayana Buddhism," a Zen friend of mine says of it—it began as a democratizing protestant sect aimed at the common people, and it accounts for some aspects of Issa's sensibility.

Poems

The poems are arranged in no particular order. Roughly chronological presentations of Issa can be found in Lewis Mackenzie, *The Autumn Wind*, and in the first volume of Blyth's *History of Haiku*.

Page 153

NEW YEAR'S DAY: Under the old calendar, the New Year began in early February and was the official beginning of spring. In this poem Issa uses the phrase *medetasamo*, "congratulations," or "Happy New Year." So the poem could be translated: "Happy New Year! / About average / my spring."

Page 155

CLIMB MOUNT FUJI: This is Blyth's translation slightly rearranged. He takes the view that the poem doesn't exhort perseverance—which, for him, would make it didactic and therefore not a haiku—but observes a creature acting from its own nature.

Page 156

THE MAN PULLING RADISHES: The radishes are *daikon*, which look like long, skinny turnips.

MOON, PLUM BLOSSOMS: Issa uses an idiom, *su no konyaku no,* which Blyth renders as "all at sixes and sevens." *Su* is vinegar, *konyaku* is soy paste. I wanted to convey the idiom, but an attractive translation might be:

> Moon, blossoms,
> vinegar, soy paste,
> and there goes the day.

ASKED HOW OLD HE WAS: New Year's is the first day of spring, and everyone's birthday. Issa is noticing the span of the boy's hand—five fingers only—and feels the tug of mortality.

O OWL: This kind of humorous direct address is typical of the Danrin style. According to Mackenzie, the wife of a friend of Issa suspected this poem was about her and was mortally offended.

SEEN: According to Lucien Stryk, the use of the telescope at the teahouse near Yushima Shrine cost three cents.

DON'T KNOW ABOUT THE PEOPLE: "Scarecrow" is an autumn *kigo* and, of course, suggests mortal bareness. The folks in Kashiwabara sided with Issa's stepmother in their epic dispute over his father's property.

JANUARY: "The tree known as the Japanese apricot, to begin with an anomaly, is native to China, not Japan, its small white flowers being a favorite of Chinese painters and poets; its Latin name is *Prunus mume,* from *mume* or *ume,* the Japanese version of the Chinese name *mei;* and practically everyone outside of horticultural experts refers to it as a plum. If all of that is quite clear, I

will add that it is revered in China and Japan as a symbol of forti-
tude because it blooms in winter, before any other flower will
venture out." Burton Watson, *The Rainbow World*, p. 62. Issa
may have in mind here the fact that spring came late to his moun-
tain village.

Page 163

BLOSSOMS AT NIGHT: The white blossoms of the pear.

Page 164

THE WITHERED FIELDS: The phrase is *kareno*, and it's often trans-
lated "withered moor" because it implies uncultivated land. It's a
fall-winter seasonal phrase and Issa is playing with it here. Its as-
sociations are equivalent to the beginning of a ghost story.

Page 165

IT ONCE HAPPENED: According to Blyth, the idiom of this poem is
highly formal.

Page 167

FLOPPED ON THE FAN: A summer poem; the strategic problem is
whether to wake the cat.

Page 168

RED MORNING SKY: Slight variant on Blyth's translation.

Page 171

THAT GORGEOUS KITE: Kites are associated with spring.

Page 175

SHINANO: Issa's home province in the mountains.

DUCKS BOBBING ON THE WATER: Literally, "looking for fortune,"

---

but the phrase he uses for the "bobbing" ducks, *ukine,* would imply sleeping around. *See* Mackenzie, *The Autumn Wind,* p. 87.

Page 176

THE SIX WAYS: The title refers to the six ways of reincarnation, or the six forms of existence. Groups of haiku on the same subject, *rensakushi,* are said to have been originated by Buson.

Page 178

NO DOUBT ABOUT IT: The mountain cuckoo, or *kankadori*'s call, though stronger, resembles a dove's.

Page 179

A GOOD WORLD: Lucien Stryk's translation.

Page 183

IN A DREAM: Written after his daughter's death.

Page 184

THE CUCKOO SINGS: *Ware to yama / hawaru gawaru ni / hoto-togisu.* The "this way–that way" of *hawaru gawaru* is onomato-poeic, and it also gets a pleasing visual inflection from the slightly different ways of making the syllables for *ha-* and *ga-*.

Page 186

THESE SEA SLUGS: Issa's response to a call for patriotic poems.

Page 187

WRITING SHIT ABOUT NEW SNOW: His response to a contest on the theme "new snow" sponsored by a wealthy patron. He says, "nonsense." I tuned it up a little. The joke is that it is a perfectly correct haiku and uses the seasonal phrase "new snow," which symbolizes, of course, freshness and purity.

I ENVY: There are many poems about his sense of himself as an orphan.

Page 188

WERE IT SWEET: Blyth's translation.

Page 190

NOT KNOWING: The fish are for eating.

NEW YEAR'S MORNING: They've escaped being made a meal of.

Page 191

THE WORLD OF DEW: See, on page 228, how Issa frames this poem in *A Year of My Life*. The phrase "This is a world of dew" is a conventional piety of the Jōdo-shin sect, but it expresses a fundamental Buddhist idea. Impermanence, *mujō*, is the second of the three basic qualities of existence. The first is suffering, the third contingency. The classic Mahayana formulation appears at the end of the *Diamond Sutra:* "All conditioned things are like a dream, a phantom, a drop of dew, a lightning flash. That is how to observe them."

Page 193

WHY DID THE WILD PINK BREAK: The name of the *nadeshiko*, or pink *(Dianthus superbus)*, was written with the Chinese characters for "to comfort" and "child." The flower is, despite the name, white.

Page 195

THE MOON TONIGHT: Written after the death of his wife, Kiku.

Page 196

A BATH WHEN YOU'RE BORN: The phrase I've translated "how stupid" is *chimpunkan*, "nonsense."

Journal of My Father's Last Days

For the complete text, see the list of further readings. When Issa returned to Kashiwabara in the early spring of 1801, he was about thirty-nine years old. Huey: "In *Chichi no Shūen Nikki,* Issa says that there was no particular reason for him to return when he did, although Kobayashi Keiichiro suggests that he was probably interested in re-establishing himself in the community so that he might settle down there." Kashiwabara was a village of mountain farmers. Though Issa was a quite well-known poet and *haikai* teacher in Edo, it is not difficult to suppose that his step-mother and half brother saw him as an idler from the big city come to secure his interest in the farm they had been working for the twenty-five years he'd been away.

Though the *nikki,* or diary, was an established literary form, there had been nothing quite like Issa's detailed and realistic de-scription of his father's death. Robert Huey observes that *shūenki,* deathbed accounts of famous people, were not uncom-mon. Issa's originality was to adapt the form to his own experi-ence, a son's watch over his failing father, an obscure mountain farmer in a bitterly unhappy household. At the end of the nine-teenth century, the Japanese naturalist prose writers, looking for antecedents for their aesthetic, were particularly interested in Issa's account, and their interest is partly responsible for Issa's prestige in the twentieth century.

The tone of the journal has much to do with the importance of filial piety in Issa's culture, but I gather that even Japanese read-ers find it somewhat lugubrious. It's interesting to compare Issa's tone with that of a notorious late medieval set of linked verses. The first poet wrote:

> Bitter, bitter it was
> And yet somehow funny.

The second provided a context:

> Even as
> my father lay dying,
> I went on farting.

It makes one see that, although Issa's account of the other figures in the story reads like Balzac, the account of his own emotions is cast in a much more sentimental and idealized mode. I've indicated places where the journal is abridged with asterisks.

Page 199

FOUNDER OF OUR SECT: Shinran, 1174–1268, founded the Jōdo Shin-shū sect.

Page 200

A BLIND TORTOISE: It was said to be as unlikely, among all the forms of being, to be born a human being and therefore capable of hearing the dharma and achieving salvation as for a blind tortoise to find a piece of driftwood to cling to in the open sea.

Page 201

THREE OBLIGATIONS: For a woman, as a daughter to her father, as wife to her husband, as widow to her son.

Page 203

TWENTY-FOUR DISCIPLES: The disciples of Shinran.

Page 205

MAGICAL SKILL OF PUTTING FIRE INTO A BAG: This passage refers to miracles performed by various Chinese Taoist sages. Huey: "Issa's growing interest in the classics of Japan and China soon found its way into his work with mixed results."

Page 208

HE DOWNED FIVE GO: A go is a third of a pint. Yagohei drank about a quart of sake.

Page 211

GREAT SERPENT: Legends of women turning into serpents figured in No and Kabuki plays.

Page 212

THAT LAND: The Pure Land of the Jōdo Shin-shū sect.

AWAKO: Huey says he has not translated this word because its meaning is unknown; perhaps a local expression.

Page 213

JIVAKA, BIAN QUE; HUA TUO: Legendary physicians in classical literature.

Page 214

THE IMPERMANENT SPRING FLOWERS: The parallelism in this sentence has—and had for Issa's readers—the strong flavor of classical Chinese poetry. The quotations that follow are drawn from Japanese poetry.

Page 216

IT WAS THE SEVENTH DAY: Huey: "Relatives of the deceased would visit the grave every seven days for forty-nine days. According to Buddhist belief, the deceased is reborn into a different world every seventh day after death, until the forty-ninth day, when his fate is decided."

SIX PASSIONS: The desires for order, form, graceful movement, voice, softness, and features.

A Year of My Life

A Year of My Life, or *Ora ga Haru*—the phrase means, literally, "my spring"—was written in 1819 and seems to have been carefully revised. It has something of the flavor of an old

almanac—odds and ends of stories and legends, some of them
funny, usually morally instructive—and into it comes the ac-
count of the death of his daughter.

I've indicated with asterisks sections that I've abridged.

Page 217

RICE CAKE: *Zoni,* or rice cake with vegetables, was a traditional
New Year's dish.

Page 221

ONLY BIRDS: For another, more positive translation, *see* Early
Miner, *Japanese Linked Verse,* p. 104:

> Even in our time
> The Lotus Sutra has been sounded
> in the cry of the warbler.

Page 224

THE TOLL COLLECTORS: Toll collectors were much despised. They
are burning the wood to keep warm. Part of the point is that one
still pays toll when plums are blossoming. Yuasa describes this
poem as "ambiguous."

Page 229

A LARGE CHESTNUT TREE: See Bashō's *haibun* about the chestnut
on page 39.

BASHŌ ON POETRY

Learn from the Pine

These remarks by Bashō on poetry and poetics are drawn from
various sources—his own prose and observations reported by his
disciples—and various translators. It's not completely clear that

---

he said everything attributed to him. Bashō himself wrote no systematic treatise on poetics, and his ideas changed over time.

Page 233

LEARN ABOUT PINES: One of Bashō's students provides a gloss: "To do this you must leave your subjective preoccupation with yourself. Otherwise you impose yourself on the object and do not learn. Your poetry issues of its own accord when you and the object have become one—when you have plunged deep enough into the object to see something glimmering there. However well-phrased your poetry may be, if your feeling is not natural— if the object and yourself are separate—then your poetry is not true poetry but merely your subjective counterfeit." I've seen this statement attributed to Bashō himself in several English language sources, but as far as I know, he didn't say it. *See* Nobuyuki Yuasa, *The Narrow Road to the Far North and Other Travel Sketches,* p. 33.

DON'T FOLLOW: De Bary, *Sources of the Japanese Tradition,* p. 450.

THE BASIS OF ART: *See* Earl Miner, *Japanese Linked Verse,* p. 116.

MAKE THE UNIVERSE: R. H. Blyth, *History of Haiku,* vol. 1, pp. 13–14.

Page 234

ONE SHOULD KNOW: Makoto Ueda, *Matsuo Bashō,* p. 165.

THE SECRET OF POETRY: Source not known.

ONE MUST FIRST OF ALL: Miner, *Japanese Linked Verse,* p. 148.

SABI IS THE COLOR: Yuasa, *Narrow Road,* p. 42.

WHEN YOU ARE COMPOSING: Ueda, *Literary and Art Theories in Japan,* p. 159

COMPOSITION MUST OCCUR: Ueda, *Zeami, Bashō, Yeats, Pound* p. 52. *See* Miner: "Bashō was a slow writer, producing in a lifetime fewer stanzas than Saikaku dashed off in a single day. He would fuss over a single stanza for a long time, working on this or that line until what he sought was finally gained." *Japanese Linked Verse*, p. 94.

IS THERE ANY GOOD: Ueda, *Matsuo Bashō*, p. 162.

IN COMPOSING HOKKU: Ueda, *Zeami, Bashō*, p. 39.

Page 235

HAIKAI EXISTS: Imoto Noichi, "Independence of Hokku in Haikai and Its Significance," p. 29.

THERE ARE THREE ELEMENTS: Miner, "Bashō," p. 95. Notice that, for all his insistence on nature and plainness, Bashō by no means thinks of language as a transparent medium.

THE PROFIT OF HAIKAI: Ueda, "Bashō and the Poetics of Haiku," p. 430.

IF YOU DESCRIBE: Yuasa, *Narrow Road*, p. 24

THE HOKKU HAS CHANGED: Haruo Shirane, "Matsuo Bashō and the Poetics of Scent," p. 78.

IN THIS MORTAL FRAME: Yuasa, *Narrow Road*, p. 72.

Page 236

POETRY IS A FIREPLACE: Ueda, "Poetics," p. 423.

AFTER WANDERING: Ueda, *Matsuo Bashō*, pp. 168–69.

THERE IS A COMMON ELEMENT: Ueda, "Poetics," p. 423.

Page 237

EVERY FORM: Blyth, *History of Haiku*, vol. 1, p. 13.

WHEN WE OBSERVE: Ueda, "Poetics," p. 424.

ONE NEED NOT: Ueda, *Literary and Art Theories*, p. 165.

CLAD IN A BLACK ROBE: Yuasa, *Narrow Road,* p. 65

I ALWAYS FEEL: Imoto, "Independence of Hokku," p. 30.

IT'S ADMIRABLE: Ueda, *Matsuo Bashō,* p. 10.

SINCE ANCIENT TIMES: Ueda, *Matsuo Bashō,* p. 116

Page 238

ONE NEEDS: Ueda, *Zeami Bashō,* p. 63. My paraphrase.

THE BONES: *See* Miner, *Japanese Linked Verse,* p. 119. The terms are *sabishimi* and *okashimi*. *Okashimi* means "peculiar, humorous." *Sabishimi* is a matter of debate, related to *sabi* "refined," "objective," "solitary," etc.) and *sabishi* "lonely," so it could be translated "loneliness and humor."

A VERSE: Ueda, *Matsuo Bashō,* p. 163.

EAT VEGETABLE SOUP: Ueda, *Literary and Art Theories,* p. 166

THE STYLE: Ueda, *Literary and Art Theories,* p. 166.

THE LEAVES: Donald Shiveley, "Bashō: The Man and the Plant," pp. 158–59.

Conversations with Bashō

Mukai Kyorai (1651–1704) was born into a samurai family in Nagasaki. He gave up a military career and began to study with Bashō in 1685, and they were particularly close. In addition to editing *The Monkey's Cloak* and assembling Bashō's remarks on hokku and *haikai* in *Conversations,* he edited *Narrow Road to the Far North.* In his last years he was a *haikai* teacher in Kyoto. This work was not published until seventy years after his death.

Page 242

THE MONKEY'S CLOAK: *Sarumino,* often translated as *The Monkey's Straw Raincoat,* was published in 1691. It was one of the important anthologies of the Bashō group. It included four *kasen* and a selection of hokku.

A SKYLARK: The bird is a *hototogisu*, a cuckoo. Keene perhaps thought to translate it into a bird with similar poetic associations in the English tradition.

Page 243

IGA POETS: Iga was Bashō's home district, and he took a special interest in its poets.

Page 249

IN THE PLUM TREE: This and the following two verses are in the five syllable–five syllable form of the even-numbered verses in a *renga* sequence.

Page 250

SOMBER AND TALL: Keene, in *Sources of Japanese Tradition,* vol. 1 (p. 458), remarks, "By evoking the excitement caused by the blossoming of the cherry tree he gives a most dramatic picture of the arrival of spring in a dark wood."

A Note on *Haikai,* Hokku, and Haiku

THE term *haikai* means "sportive or playful." It came to be applied to a kind of Japanese poetry that originated in the middle ages, or earlier, called *renga. Renga* was a form of collaborative poetry, usually written by three or more poets, that was created by giving the *tanka,* the five-line poem of the classical anthologies, a sort of call-and-response form. One poet wrote a first verse of three lines in a five syllable–seven syllable–five syllable pattern, and the second poet completed the tanka with two seven-syllable lines. For example, one poet might write (I won't try to keep the syllable count):

> A great city stood here—
> now the roads lead to the past,
> there are flowers blooming.

And the second poet would finish it:

> They are gone in a second,
> the dreams of spring.

Or, since the early *renga* used an elevated diction, the fourth line might read, "How quickly they pass!"

One can imagine English Renaissance courtiers devising such a form, but the next step seems decidedly unwestern. A third poet writes another three lines, which, together with the previous couplet, make an entirely new poem:

They are gone in a second,
the dreams of spring.

Just say the word "cherry"
and it storms down the mountain,
the autumn wind.

Then the next poet adds another couplet to make a third poem, which is completely independent of the first two:

Just say the word "cherry"
and it storms down the mountain,
the autumn wind.

Yet the still dews of summer
linger on the haze-thickened moors.

And so on. The seasons change, the subject changes, and, in the classical *renga*, the poem proceeds through a hundred verses.

Rules developed. The *renga* had to be written in a certain way. No story could be developed, the seasons had to keep changing, a traditional image of the autumn moon had to be introduced at least twice, images of spring flowers three times, and so on. The form became immensely popular among educated people at court and in the monasteries. Treatises were written on appropriate ways of making links, and anthologies of examples were published. Sometimes the form was taken quite seriously; sometimes it was the pretext for a drinking party. The tone and subject matter, were elevated, though a form of comic *renga* developed. And it began to spread, as a social activity, to cities and towns, and was taken up by merchants and farmers, some of whom were imitating the refinements of the court, some of whom were drawn to it from the learned traditions of the monastery.

These *renga* often used a more informal language, treated their subjects playfully, and were shorter, often thirty-six verses long. The thirty-six-verse form was called a *kasen*, and the style of the poetry was called *haikai no renga*. Here, loosely rendered, is an example, from the middle of a *kasen* by Bashō's group. The first poet begins with a three-line verse:

> Riding
> a three-year-old pony
> in the early fall.

The second poet adds:

> Rain falling
> every which way.

The third poet turns the hard fall rain into a summer shower:

> Dusk—
> they're packed in
> the hot spring bath of Suma.

The next poet completes this scene:

> In among them—
> a wandering priest.

The next leaves who the "them" is vague, and creates another scene altogether:

> Pushing
> the talk
> in one direction only.

A group of people, perhaps in the city, a lay priest going on about religion. The next poet dissolves the obsessive preacher into an obsessive lover:

Started by chance,
their love gets serious.

This couplet involves a pun. It could read: "Hungry, love
gets violent." And the next poet, taking the pun for a cue,
alters the scene:

"Eat something,"
the mother says,
"you'll get over him."

And the next softens and romanticizes the love-struck girl:

The sleeves of the moon-gazers
have grown wet with dew.

The dew is autumn dew. The next poet takes a hint from
the seasons and presents a harvest-moon-viewing party
disrupted by a storm:

Boat in the wind—
she's frightened
by the sound of the waves.

And so on. Schools developed that were also social clubs
for people who wanted to learn to participate, and there
were established masters who supervised the proceedings,
accepting some verses and rejecting others, discussing is-
sues of craft and sensibility.

Bashō, Buson, and Issa were all, at different times in
their lives, *haikai* masters. When they went to the city as
young men to learn their art, *haikai no renga* was the art
they went to learn. The three-line verse that began a *renga*
was called a *hokku*. It was not thought of as an individual
poem. Or not exactly. It had a special place of prestige in
the sequence, admirable hokku were known and recited,
and part of *renga* training in Bashō's time involved training

in the writing of hokku. The anthologies of Bashō's group were typically sequences of *kasen,* sometimes followed by a selection of individual hokku by members of the group, organized not by individual author but by the season of the year. In addition, in his travel journals, Bashō recorded some of his own hokku and those of his friends and worked toward shaping the combination of prose and closing hokku verse into its own poetic form, *haibun,* a practice he brought to its highest development in the carefully revised *Narrow Road to the Far North* and the later *Saga Diary.*

By Buson's time, the hokku—partly because of the brilliance of Bashō's work in the form, partly because the printing press had made the *renga* much less a private, social occasion—came to be seen as a somewhat more independent entity. As Mark Morris puts it in "Buson and Shiki: Part One", "when Buson and his friends and students got together, it was usually to compose hokku on themes selected on the spot or to compare and evaluate poems they had made earlier, again on set traditional topics. That is, the overall trend was toward haikai as the writing of individual poems, but not yet as the poetry of individuals." (p. 382) Bashō is reported to have said, in an uncharacteristic moment of self-approval, that one of his students may have excelled him at hokku, but that no one could better the old man at *haikai.* Buson, on the other hand, was aware of being much better at hokku that at *haikai;* the best of his *haikai* sequences was written by him and one friend, and it was much revised in correspondence. In his last years Buson copied about fifteen hundred of his hokku into copybooks, apparently cleaning up his personal literary legacy, but almost all the work printed in his lifetime appeared in the context of group anthologies of *haikai* and hokku.

By Issa's time the hokku form was still more independent, though he was also a *haikai* master. Issa published most of his poems in a series of journals that contained hokku, a few tanka and Chinese poems, and short essays on places he'd visited and events that caught his eye. The changing attitude toward the independence of the short poem is reflected in the production of the poets. Bashō wrote approximately a thousand hokku, Buson three thousand, Issa something like twenty thousand. Around Issa's time the term *haiku* was coined, collapsing *haikai* and *hokku*, but it was not until the time of Shiki in the 1890s that our conception of haiku was in place as an independent art form severed from the old context of *haikai* practice.

Those old contexts are striking in many ways, both strange and familiar. First, there are the form and content of the *renga* itself. The nearest thing to its sudden shifts and dissolves in the western tradition is probably early surrealist film: shot of a woman in a summer garden; shot of a man opening a gate; shot of the man wrestling a moose; shot of a referee blowing a whistle; shot of a football being kicked off; shot of the woman catching the football, etc. And there are a few modernist poets whose individual works come near to the *renga* spirit, at least in part: Ezra Pound's experiments with metamorphosis in his *Draft of XXX Cantos,* for example, or nearer yet, Wallace Stevens's "Thirteen Ways of Looking at a Blackbird," or, more recently, a work that combines something of Stevens with something of French surrealism, such as John Ashbery's *Three Poems.* But these seem, implicitly or explicitly, techniques in search of a worldview. And the old films like Buñuel's and Dalí's *Andalusian Dog* and René Clair's *Entr'acte* were assaults on the master narrative of their time through which European society constructed a world that made sense. But in the Buddhist tradition the view of the world implied by *renga* made perfect sense and was deeply shared. (p. 321) As medieval poet Nijo Yoshimoto put it, "Renga is not exhausted by the meaning of the stanza that precedes or of the stanza that follows, nor yet by prosperity or decline, grief or happiness; for just as we set boundaries only to have them shift away, so there is nothing in this transient world. As we consider today, it has grown tomorrow. As we consider spring, it has become autumn. As we consider the flowers, they have faded to yellow leaves. Is it not all summed up in 'swirling petals and falling leaves'?" (Earl Miner, Japanese *Linked Poetry*, p. 39) *Renga* was a way of enacting the contingency—and, therefore, the unreality—of all natural things.

Most accounts of *renga* in English language sources tend to dismiss it as an aristocratic parlor game, like whist or bridge, from which haiku, conceived as an imagist or romantic art, emerged. There is some evidence for this view. "If a hokku is poorly composed," one fourteenth-century treatise says solemnly, "the whole poetry party will be spoilt." And there was a good deal of triviality and buffoonery in many of the later *renga* sessions, but *renga* came from deep sources in Japanese Buddhist culture. Its sudden shifts not only reflected the basic Buddhist belief, as one scholar put it, "that universes originate, develop, change, and perish through the operation of natural causes, and that this cyclic process has no beginning or end," it was also a way of entering a right relationship to those processes.

Here is how another fourteenth-century treatise puts it: "...contemplating deeply the vicissitudes of the life of man and body, always keep in your heart the image of *mujo* (ephemerality), and when you go to the mountains or the sea, feel the pathos *(aware)* of the karma of sentient beings and non-sentient things. Give feeling to those things without a heart *(mushintai no mono)* and through your own heart express their beauty *(yūgen)* in a delicate form. Through the four seasons of the plants and trees, feel the truth of 'swirling petals and falling leaves,' being enlightened by the changes of birth, old age, illness, and death.... " (Gary Ebersole, "Matsuo Bashō and the Way of Poetry in the Japanese Religious Tradition," pp. 514–15). This connects to and in some way clarifies the sources of Bashō's attitude in the more practical instruction he gave his students two hundred years later: "In kasen there should be no desire to retrace even one step. As the series progresses, it brings renewal to our hearts, and this is only because of the consciousness that does not look back, that pushes the movement forward."

Another striking difference between *haikai* and western art is the matter of poetry as a communal activity. Mark Morris describes it in his essay on Buson: "... in Buson's time haikai generally and hokku as well were as much activities as literary forms. Haikai was something you did, not simply a means of production of texts, or the texts themselves. One engaged in haikai through a personal relationship with haikai's past as embodied in one's teacher. You joined a group or groups, and while book study was an important part of your integration into haikai (that it might speak better through you), much of the learning and enjoyment took place in the face-to-face interaction with your teacher and fellow poets. Shop owner, priest, samurai, actor, wealthy farmer, or petty bureaucrat, the poet was provided with a vantage point on the old poetry and a style growing from it contingent upon his teacher and his haikai ancestry. You belonged to all that and it to you, and what's more, the government could neither tax it nor take it away. Several centuries of the manufacture of haikai were sustained and propelled by two by-products that were for many poets probably more important than what appeared concretely on the page: wit and pleasure." And, one could add, a context for the expression of the part of yourself daily life didn't call upon, and a community in which to refine and express it.

Parts of this description are familiar enough: the master–apprentice relationship, the schools of poets with shared aesthetic ideals who reinforce and provide an audience for one another's work. The part that remains strange is the *renga* itself. There is nothing quite like this collaborative and improvisatory activity in the western literary tradition. The nearest thing to it, perhaps—a group of artists who get together to perform, improvising on one another's themes within a context that is, in the end, concerned with the group production, under the direction of a master—is the American jazz band of the 1920s. There are other similarities, too: a popular medium, reverence for masters, styles, soloists of the past, rival styles in the same city, different traditions in different cities, travel and performance as a means of spreading a group's style, and art as an expression of freedom, without isolation, in a very limiting social context. In this way, if in no other, the nearest thing to Bashō's hokku in the West in the twentieth century is Louis Armstrong's solo in "Tight Like That" or "Potato Head Blues."

A Note on Translation

Most of the verse translations are mine. In a few cases I thought that other translations—by R. H. Blyth, Sam Hamill, Lucien Stryk, Makoto Ueda, and Jorie Graham —could not be bettered and I've indicated those in the notes.

Over twenty years ago, reading R. H. Blyth, I began to make my own versions of his translations, from an impulse to simplify or clarify them as a way of saying to myself what I saw in the poems. Eventually, I acquired grammars and dictionaries and set myself to the task of parsing, decoding, and making a version of one haiku per day. In this way, though my starting point was almost always a previous scholarly translation, I got a little closer to the Japanese originals and their swift, laconic syntax, and over the years, learning a little—very little— Japanese as I went, I made a hundred or so versions each of poems by Bashō, Buson, and Issa.

I've tried to be faithful in the sense that I've added nothing to the poets' own words, except in the few cases where I was trying to convey the effect of a pun. There are many puns in the originals. And countless literary allusions and subtle variations on literary allusions. One can get a sense of the way the punning, made possibly by the large number of homonyms in the Japanese language, works, by looking at a little song from Shake-speare:

> Golden lads and girls all must,
> As chimney-sweepers, come to dust.

The lines take on additional poignance if you know that "golden lad" was an Elizabethan name for dandelions and that the nimbus of dried seeds was called a "chimney-sweep." Mostly, if I've recognized the puns in the poems or been clued to them by scholarly commentary, I've either annotated them or ignored them. If I saw a way to bring across clearly one part of what the poem was doing, I was more than grateful to settle for that.

Here is a short survey of other features of these poems that make them untranslatable.

SYNTAX

The swiftness of the syntax is one of the fascinating things about these poems, and I don't think it can be rendered. The poem by Issa, for example, that I translated as follows:

> In this world
> we walk on the roof of hell
> gazing at flowers.

looks like this in the original:

> *Yo no naka wa / jigoku no ue no / hanami kana*

world's middle as-for / hell's top's / flower viewing!

It's very fast, and I think a more accurate translation

> This world: hell's roof's flower viewing

goes by too quickly to make a poem in English.

Rhythm

There is no stress rhythm in Japanese, since each syllable is spoken at more or less the same pitch, but the flow of the phrases and pauses creates a rhythm, particularly in the second seven-syllable unit. Bashō typically patterns his pauses about midway through the second unit, so the rhythm of the poem is 5-4-3-5 or 5-3-4-5, which has a rather balanced effect. Buson very often introduces the pause into the second line earlier or later, 5-5-2-5 or 5-2-5-5, which creates a much more emphatic effect. Buson is also much more inclined to do without the *kireji*, or cutting word that's usually translated as punctuation—autumn moon *dash*, spring blossoms *colon*—and so he uses more enjambment. It's almost never possible to render the first of these effects, and not always the second.

Chinese Characters

Japanese is written in a combination of phonetic signs for individual syllable sounds and ideograms based on Chinese characters, or *kanji*. From the beginning the *haikai* poets, though they used the common language and the phonetic syllabary, also used *kanji*. This made a lot of allusive echoing possible and some metaphorical intensification. For example, Bashō, in "This road / no one goes down it / autumn evening," uses the Chinese character for "road," *michi*, which is *tao* in Chinese, and immediately enlarges the metaphor of the poem; and Issa in a poem about his son's death, writes the word for a wildflower, "pink," in Chinese characters that, read separately, mean "child" and "to comfort." These effects obviously can't be rendered in

English. Buson especially uses a lot of ideograms. Mark Morris describes it as "sinifying the look and direction of haikai." (See "Buson and Shiki: Part One," p. 422) Morris examines a particular poem in which the first five syllables are written in phonetic signs, the next seven in the Chinese characters for the individual words, and the next five in the phonetic signs again, and describes the effect as that of Chinese rain falling on a Japanese landscape. Buson sometimes made suggestions for revision to his students based not on what a word meant but on how it looked. Such visual nuances are not in the range of an English translation.

PIVOT WORDS

Pivot words, *kake-kotoba*, are a peculiar feature of Japanese poetry. They are words that suddenly change the meaning, or the expectation of meaning, of a sentence, as you read it, a kind of grammatical double exposure. In this poem for a recent American literary magazine—

> You despised my heart-
> sick letter. Probably rightly—

"heart-sick" is a kind of *kake-kotoba*. Two examples from Buson, both discussed by Mark Morris in "Buson and Shiki: Part One" are:

> *hototogisu / matsu ya miyako no / soradanome*
>
> cuckoo / I await: the city's / empty hopes

> *zetchō no / shiro tanomoshiki / wakaba kana*
>
> fortress's / heights peaceful / young leaves!

The first of these poems looks straightforward enough, but the phrase *miyako no sora* means "city sky," or, since *miyako* means "metropolis" or "capital," "the sky of the capital." So the two phrases, "the city's empty hopes" and "the city sky" are in effect superimposed on one another. Hence Mark Morris's paraphrase:

> For the cuckoo I wait
> beneath the vain skies of hoping
> here in the capital

I would have been inclined to translate it:

> Listening
> for the cuckoo: the city's
> empty sky

and let go what Morris is trying to get, the way in which the *kake-kobata* permits Japanese poets to create the equivalent of English metaphysical conceits in a very condensed space.

In the second poem, *tanomoshiki* belongs grammatically to *wakaba*, "peaceful young leaves," but the impression on first reading is that one is going to get *tanomoshii* modifying *zetchō no shiro*, "fortress on the peaceful heights" or "fortress on the heights gives a feeling of security." In a sleight of hand Buson sets up an expectation that the fortress on the heights gives the feeling of safety and then takes it away; it's the fresh green of spring that makes us feel peaceful. Again Morris offers a paraphrase: "Fresh green of the trees to rest the heart, to hold firm the fort on the hilltop." Another translation takes a different strategy and leaves out the surprise altogether:

> Crowning the summit,
> majestically it stands,
> a castle among green leaves.

Add to this difficulty the fact that for "fortress" Buson chose the Chinese compound *zetchō* rather than the Japanese *itadaki*, and you see the problem. Its harsh sound, as Shiki observed, provides a stronger contrast with *wakaba*, "young leaves," a spring *kigo* that implies a tender freshness. Perhaps,

> Old fortress on the heights
> and the freshness
> of young leaves.

But the interest of the poem, what saves it from static picturesqueness, is only conveyed by Morris's quite long paraphrase.

SEASONAL WORDS

Kigo, or seasonal phrases, are the essence of haiku and in one way simple enough to translate. But, as Mark Morris observes, "translation cannot convey the feeling of at-homeness, of being inserted in the cycle of a natural and ritual calendar that *kigo* communicate to the haikai reader." My personal theory, not especially well-informed, about *kigo* is that their origin is shamanic, animist, and ritualistic, that the words for "winter blast" and "spring blossoms" and "summer shower" were intended at one time to call forth the living spirits manifested in those natural phenomena. American poets began to take an interest in haiku around the same time at which they became interested in the translation of Native American songs, and the similarity between them was often noted. I think the reason is that they bear the traces of a similar function. The Chippewa hunter's song, soliciting the spirit of the deer, is not very different from the Japanese poet soliciting the spirit of the cherry blossoms. The shaman's songs passed into folk songs; the folk songs provided the basis for a courtly poetic tradition, on the one hand, and for a Buddhist poetic tradition, on the other. In the courtly tradition, the traditional symbols of the seasons became psychological, ways of expressing states of desire for tanka poets such as Komachi and Shikibu. In the priestly tradition of poets such as Saigyō, they became instruments of Buddhist meditation on the reality and unreality of the phenomenal world. And in the culture they became the basis, as Morris said, for a calendar of festivals, a liturgy of the seasons that told people, both high and low, how they were at home in the world and what powers they moved among.

Bashō has called attention to this process:

> The beginning of art—
> a rice-planting song
> in the backcountry.

The word I've translated "art" is *fūryū* and it also means "elegance, refinement" and calls to mind specifically the manners of the court. This is the transformation of magic into aesthetics. But the focus of the transformation of the *kigo* was Buddhism, particularly the idea of *mujō*, the transience or mutability of things. In this idea the aesthetic and the religious are joined in Japanese culture. The cherry blossoms, associated anciently with the orchard, the fertility cycle, and the priapic spring, became, in their beauty and briefness, poignant emblems of the transience of the world, and this was in Buddhism a religious thought. Thus *fūryū*, the court, and by extension Japanese society, and *mujō*, insight into the transitoriness of the world from which the path to enlightenment begins, and *oku*, the backcountry, the old magic of the furrow and the seed, are joined in a single image, and together they make a whole culture.

From the point of view of poetry, time is the crucial element here. The *haikai* and haiku anthologies were usually organized seasonally: spring, summer, fall, winter. They were, and still are, magical and ritual accounts of the Japanese year. At the same time—and this is one of the tensions at the heart of the form—they are a record of the evanescence of all being. Buson expresses this tension between the comfort of magical, cyclical time and the self-erasing linear time, which, in Buddhism, is to be transcended, in this poem where, as is often the case, he has it both ways:

> The old calendar
> fills me with gratitude
> like a sutra.

Zen complicates this issue further by putting such pressure on the moment of perception. Cycles and their passing can be experienced collectively through common cultural symbols, but only individual persons experience moments. Though haiku has been presented in the West as a unique expression of Zen, none of the three great poets in the tradition was, formally, a Zen Buddhist. Only Bashō seems to have studied it seriously, and that for a short time. But all three of them read intensely in classical Chinese poetry, and both Buson and Issa studied Bashō. And there is not much doubt that it is something like the Zen habit of mind that led Bashō in the early 1680s to transform the *haikai* tradition, and to create a style that eventually turned the *hokku* into the *haiku*, a poem centered in an individual human consciousness. I believe that this is something that came to him through the literary tradition, through Chinese poets like Tu Fu, and through the priestly tradition in the poetry of Sōgi and Saigyō, rather than from formal religious training. In any case, it was crucial. It added to, or imposed on, the ideas of cyclical time and linear time the no time of Zen Buddhism. In Bashō's best poems, each individual moment of perception is all there is—or what there is, and at the same time, it isn't anything at all. There are different ways to say this, or parts of it—the world really seen is the world; every moment is eternal; or, every moment of time is all time; therefore time doesn't exist. In any case, after Bashō, the genius of the form is the way in which, through trained perception, it compresses the experiences of cyclical time, linear time, and the all time–no time of Zen into seventeen syllables.

The *kigo* is the focus of this compression. The subtleties of the *kigo*—that the *uguisu*, or bush warbler, is the harbinger of spring, that the *hotogisu*, or little cuckoo, is a bird of early summer, the *kankadori*, or Himalayan cuckoo, a bird of midsummer, that *harusame*, "spring rain," is the rain of the first and second months, *haru no ame*, "rain of spring," the rain of the second and third months—is bound to be lost on most readers in English, as it is lost on most modern urban Japanese. The full weight of these terms is simply not translatable. But the experience of time, of being-in-time, that they evoke, since it's the fundamental human experience, should be there for anyone who reads the poems carefully.

Further Reading

On Haiku and Japanese Literature

Blyth, R. H. *Haiku.* 4 vols. Tokyo: Hokuseido Press, 1949–52.
———. *History of Haiku.* 2 vols. Tokyo: Hokuseido Press, 1963–64.
Henderson, Harold G. *An Introduction to Haiku.* New York Doubleday, 1958.
Ichikawa, Sanki, ed. *Haikai and Haiku.* Tokyo: Nippon Gakajutsu Shinkokai, 1958.
Keene, Donald. *Landscapes and Portraits: Appreciations of Japanese Culture.* Palo Alto and Tokyo: Kodansha International, 1971.
———. *World within Walls: Japanese Literature of the Pre-Modern Era 1600–1867.* New York: Holt, Rinehart & Winston, 1976.
McKinnon, Richard N. "Tanka and Haiku: Some Aspects of Classical Japanese Poetry." In *Indiana University Conference on Oriental–Western Literary Relations, Papers,* pp. 67–87. University of North Carolina Studies in Comparative Literature, vol. 13. Chapel Hill: University of North Carolina Press, 1955.
Miner, Earl. *Japanese Poetic Diaries.* Berkeley: University of California Press, 1969.
———. *Japanese Linked Verse: An Account with Translations of Renga and Haikai Sequences.* Princeton: Princeton University Press, 1979.

Noichi, Imoto. "Independence of Hokku in Haikai and Its Significance." *Acta Asiatica,* no. 7 (1964): 20–35.

Ueda, Makoto. *Literary and Art Theories in Japan.* Cleveland: Western Reserve University Press, 1967.

Watson, Burton. *The Rainbow World: Japan in Essays and Translations.* Seattle: Broken Moon Press, 1990.

Yasuda, Kenneth. *The Japanese Haiku: Its Essential Nature, History, and Possibilities in English.* Tokyo: Tuttle, 1958.

On Bashō

Translations

Bly, Robert. *Bashō: Poems.* San Francisco: Mudra, 1972.

Corman, Cid. *One Man's Moon: 50 Haiku by Bashō.* Frankfort, Ky.: Gnomon Press, 1984.

Corman, Cid and Susumu, Kamaike. *Back Roads to Far Towns: Bashō's Oku-no-Hosomichi.* New York: Grossman, 1967.

Hamill, Sam. *Narrow Road to the Interior.* Boston: Shambala, 1991.

Keene, Donald. *Anthology of Japanese Literature.* New York: Grove, 1955.

Sato, Hiroaki and Watson, Burton. *From the Country of Eight Islands: An Anthology of Japanese Poetry.* Seattle: University of Washington Press, 1981.

Stryk, Lucien. *On Love and Barley: Haiku by Bashō.* London: Penguin Books, 1985.

Terasaki, Etsuko. "The Saga Diary of Matsuo Bashō: Introduction and Translation." *Literature East and West* 15–16 (1971): 701–18.

Ueda, Makoto. *Bashō and His Interpreters: Selected Hokku with Commentary.* Palo Alto: Stanford University Press, 1991.

Yuasa, Nobuyuki. *The Narrow Road to the Far North and Other Travel Sketches.* London: Penguin Books, 1966.

Studies

Aitken, Robert. *A Zen Wave: Bashō's Haiku and Zen.* New York and Tokyo: Weatherhill, 1978.

Ebersole, Gary L. "Matsuo Bashō and the Way of Poetry in the Japanese Religious Tradition." Ph.D. thesis, University of Chicago, Divinity School, 1981.

Foard, James H. "The Loneliness of Matsuo Bashō." *The Biographical Process.* Edited by Frank C. Reynolds and Donald Capps. The Hague: Mouton, 1976. 363–91.

Fujikawa, Fumiko. "The Influence of Tu Fu on Bashō." *Monumenta Nipponica* 20, no. 3–4 (1965): 374–88.

Hamill, Sam. *Bashō's Ghost.* Seattle: Broken Moon Press, 1989.

Keene, Donald. "Bashō's Diaries." *Travelers of a Hundred Ages,* pp. 287–320. New York: Henry Holt & Co., 1989.

La Fleur, William R. *The Karma of the Word.* Berkeley: University of California Press, 1983.

Mayhew, Lenore. *Monkey's Raincoat: Linked Poetry of the Bashō School, with Haiku Selections,* Rutland, Vt.: Tuttle, 1985.

Miner, Earl. "Bashō" *Textual Analysis: Some Readers Reading.* Edited by Mary Anne Caws. New York: Modern Language Association, 1986.

Miner, Earl, and Hiroko, Odagiri. *The Monkey's Straw Raincoat: And Other Poetry of the Bashō School.* Princeton: Princeton University Press, 1981.

Ogata, Tsutomi. "Five Methods of Appreciating Bashō's Haiku." *Acta Asiatica* 28 (1975): 42–61.

Pilgrim, Richard B. "The Religio-Aesthetic of Matsuo Bashō." *The Eastern Buddhist,* n.s. 10, no. 1 (May 1977): 35–53.

Sato, Hiroaki. *One Hundred Frogs: From Renga to Haiku in English.* New York and Tokyo: Weatherhill, 1983.

Shirane, Haruo. "Matsuo Bashō and the Poetics of Scent." *Harvard Journal of Asiatic Studies* 52, no. 1 (June 1992): 77–111.

Shively, Donald H. "Bashō: The Man and the Plant." *Harvard Journal of Asiatic Studies* 16, no. 1–2 (June 1953): 146–61.

Terasaki, Etsuko. " '*Hatsushigure*': A Linked Verse Sequence by

Bashō and His Disciples." *Harvard Journal of Asiatic Studies* 36 (1976): 204–39.

Ueda, Makoto. "Bashō and the Poetics of Haiku." *Journal of Aesthetics and Art Criticism* 21 (Summer 1963): 423–31.

———. *Zeami, Bashō, Yeats, Pound: A Study in Japanese and English Poetics.* The Hague: Mouton, 1965.

———. *Matsuo Bashō.* New York: Twayne, 1970.

———. *Bashō and His Interpreters: Selected Hokku with Commentary.* Palo Alto: Stanford University Press, 1991.

On Buson

Translations

Sato, Hiroaki and Watson, Burton. *From the Country of Eight Islands: An Anthology of Japanese Poetry.* Seattle: University of Washington Press, 1981.

Sawa, Yuki and Shiffert, Edith M. *Haiku Master Buson.* Union City, Calif.: Heian, 1978.

Studies of Buson the Painter

Cahill, James. *Scholar Painters of Japan: The Nanga School.* New York: Asia Society, 1972.

French, Calvin L. *The Poet-Painters: Buson and His Followers.* Ann Arbor: The University of Michigan Museum of Art, 1974.

Papapavlou, Cleopatra. "The Haiga Figure as a Vehicle of Buson's Ideals: With Emphasis on the Illustrated Sections of *Oku no Hosomichi* and *Nozarashi Kiko.*" Ph.D. thesis, University of California at Berkeley, 1981.

Watson, William. *Yosa-no-Buson.* London: Faber and Faber, 1960.

Yoshiho, Yonezawa and Chu, Yoshizawa. *Japanese Painting in the Literati Style.* New York and Tokyo: Weatherhill/Heibonsha, 1974.

Morris, Mark. "Buson and Shiki: Part One." *Harvard Journal of Asiatic Studies* 44, no. 1: 381–425.

———. "Buson and Shiki: Part Two." *Harvard Journal of Asiatic Studies* 45, no. 1: 257–321.

Ueda, Makoto. "Buson and the Language of Japanese Poetry." In *Essays in Japanese Literature,* edited by Katsuhiko Takeda. Waseda University Press, 1977.

Yasuhara, Eri Fujita. "Buson and Haishi: A Study of Free-Form Haikai Poetry in Eighteenth Century Japan." Ph.D. thesis, University of California at Los Angeles, 1983.

Zolbrod, Leon. "Talking Poetry: Buson's View of the Art of Haiku." *Literature East and West* 15–16 (December 1971–June 1972): 719–34.

———. "Death of a Poet-Painter: Yosa Buson's Last Year, 1783–84." In *Indo-Celtica: Gedachtnisschrift für Alf Sommerfelt,* edited by Herbert Pilch and Joachim Thurow, pp. 146–54. Munich: Max Heuber, 1972.

———. "Buson's Poetic Ideals: The Theory and Practice of Haikai in the Age of Revival, 1771–84." *Journal of Association of Teachers of Japanese* 9, no. 1 (January 1974): 1–20.

———. "Emblems of Aging and Immortality in the Poetry and Painting of Buson (1716–84)." *Selecta: Journal of the Pacific Northwest Council on Foreign Languages* 7 (1986): 26–31.

———. "The Busy Year: Buson's Life and Work, 1777." *Transactions of the Asiatic Society of Japan* 3 (1988): 53–81.

On Issa

Translations

Bly, Robert. *Ten Poems of Issa.* Moose Lake, Minn.: Robert Bly, 1969.

Mackenzie, Lewis. *The Autumn Wind: A Selection from the*

Poems of Issa. Tokyo and New York: Kodansha, 1984. Originally published by John Murray, London, 1957.

Sato, Hiroaki and Watson, Burton. *From the Country of Eight Islands: An Anthology of Japanese Poetry.* Seattle: University of Washington Press, 1981.

Stryk, Lucien. *The Dumpling Field: Haiku of Issa.* Athens, Ohio: Ohio University Press, Swallow, 1991.

Williams, C. K. *The Lark, the Thrush, and the Starling: Poems from Issa.* Providence, R.I.: Burning Deck Press, 1983.

Yuasa, Nobuyuki. *The Year of My Life: A Translation of Issa's Oraga Haru.* Berkeley: University of California Press, 1960.

Studies

Bickerton, Max. "Issa's Life and Poetry." *Transactions of the Asiatic Society of Japan,* 2d ser. 9 (1932): 111–54.

Huey, Robert N. "Journal of My Father's Last Days: Issa's *Chichi no Shuen Nikki.*" *Monumenta Nipponica,* 29, no. 1 (Spring 1984): 25–54. Includes a complete translation of the journal.

Acknowledgments

I NEED to acknowledge some debts: to Phil Dow who introduced me to R. H. Blyth's work over twenty years ago and with whom, at that time, I first collaborated on a book like this one; to R. H. Blyth, indispensible to students of haiku, and to Makoto Ueda for his invaluable work on Bashō which has so informed my sense of him, and especially for the texts and translations in his *Bashō and his Interpreters*, a book which anyone interested in the haiku form should run out and buy; to Mark Morris for his brilliant essay on Buson; to Yuki Sawa and Edith Shiffert on whose texts and translations of Buson I depended; to Eri Fujita Yasuhara for her study of Buson's long poems; to Lewis Mackenzie for Japanese texts and translations of Issa; to Cid Corman and Lucien Stryk for their translations, and to Cid Corman also for his inventive and original translation of Bashō's *Narrow Road;* to Sam Hamill for *Bashō's Ghost;* to William La Fleur and Gary Ebersole for their scholarship; and to Robert Aitken for his work on Bashō and for a memorable afternoon's conversation about Bashō some fifteen years ago in the Berkeley hills.

I had indispensible bibliographic help from Tony Barnstone, and from Stratis Haviaris of the Lamont Library at Harvard University. Thanks also to readers of the manuscript, Stephen Mitchell, Dean Young, Leif Hass,

Margaret Handley, and Brenda Hillman; and to my editor Dan Halpern. I hope the scholars and translators whose work I have meddled with to make this book will take it, despite its presumptions and its errors, as an act of homage and gratitude.

Copyright Acknowledgments

About the Editor

ROBERT HASS is the author of four books of poems, *Field Guide* (1973), *Praise* (1979), *Human Wishes* (1989) and *Sun Under Wood* (1996). He is the recipient of the William Carlos Williams Award for *Praise*, and two National Book Critics Circle Awards, in criticism for *Twentieth Century Pleasures: Prose on Poetry*, and in poetry for *Sun Under Wood*. His many other honors include fellowships from the John D. and Catherine T. MacArthur Foundation and the Guggenheim Foundation, an award of merit from the American Academy of Arts and Letters, and the PEN award for translation. In 1995 he was selected by the Library of Congress as Poet Laureate of the United States. Robert Hass teaches at the University of California, Berkeley.